Into The Mist

Journey Into Dementia

Kathleen Beard

WestBow
PRESS
A DIVISION OF THOMAS NELSON

WestBow Press books may be ordered through booksellers or by contacting:

WestBow Press
A Division of Thomas Nelson
1663 Liberty Drive
Bloomington, IN 47403
www.westbowpress.com
1-(866) 928-1240

Wayne Ewing, _Tears in God's Bottle: Reflections on Alzheimer's Caregiving_ Whitestone Circle Press, Tucson, AZ, 1999, p. 15

Scripture quotations marked KJV are taken from the King James Version of the Bible.

Scripture quotations marked NASB are taken from the New American Standard Bible®, Copyright © The Lockman foundation 1960, 1962, 1963, 1968, 1971, 1973, 1975, 1995. Used by permission.

Scripture quotations marked NKJV are taken from the New King James Version © 1982 by Thomas Nelson, Inc. Used by permission. All rights reserved.

Scripture quotations marked AMP are taken from the Amplified Bible, ©1965 by Zondervan Publishing House, Grand Rapids, Michigan. Used by Permission.

ISBN: 978-1-4497-1207-5 (sc)
ISBN: 978-1-4497-1209-9 (e)
Library of Congress Control Number: 2011921675
Printed in the United States of America
WestBow Press rev. date:2/28/2011

Lovingly and adoringly dedicated to John M. Beard, "My Bear"

Contents

Acknowledgements

To attempt to name every beloved person who has contributed to the perfecting of my walk with Jesus Christ would require a book all its own. Therefore, though I name some whose support and encouragement were lent to me for the writing of this book, it is not to ignore the many whose love, encouragement and support have contributed to every detail of the living water that continues to flow from their lives into mine and hopefully into the lives of others.

I thank my sons, Adam and Dane Chinnock and their loving wives, Jeniece and Tasha, for their constant comfort during John's illness. Their prayers and encouragement kept my arms from hanging limp and my knees from growing weak. How many times did Adam stop whatever he was doing to pray for me or bolster my faith when I was too overwhelmed to pray for myself. Dane, who added to my faith with a quiet understanding and practical help, and for the really difficult things he was called upon to do in John's last days. God richly blessed me with sons who know Him and serve Him. To all of my precious "kidlets," my grandchildren whose wide-eyed innocence, bubbly smiles and constant hugs, provided a constant reminder of the cycle of life; they were my future, my reason for pressing on.

I thank my Mom, Inez Shannon, who called out to a God she did not know as a young child and has followed faithfully from that day forward. Her prayer life is one I desire to model but so far have managed to barely touch; for her prayers have sustained me in innumerable ways. I learned the value of prayer from my Mom. If my Mom tells you she will pray for you, she will pray for you until that prayer is answered or you are gone from this earth. Her unconditional love models the love of Jesus Christ and I am so grateful that I discovered that while I could still thank her and appreciate her.

I thank my sisters, Linda Snyder and Pat Lutz who in their own giftings of the Holy Spirit, came alongside me at just the right moments to offer just the right Scripture, prayer, or encouragement. I cannot begin to express my appreciation for this. Each of you in your own unique identity in Christ offered exactly what Jesus would have offered if He had been talking to me on the phone, bringing me down from panic and fear.

I thank the other members of my family; my nephews and nieces and their wives and husbands. There is nothing like family and I thank God for the amazing family He has given to me. Thanks for the many ways you all stepped up to the plate to take the burden from me.

I thank Diana Taylor, whose influence in my life began a long time ago, as she was used by God to nudge me back to Him after I had walked away in discouragement. We have been through so many difficult and amazing journeys together that I sit and marvel at how God has used her in my life. Not the least of which has been her urging me to write this book, getting me to my first writer's conference even when I protested that I was not a writer, and introducing me to Donna Goodrich who did the first editing. So, here we are friend, on another wild ride together.

I thank Guy and Diane Naus, who introduced me to the Abiding Life Ministries and who held my hand and mentored me along the road of discovery that "you never know that Jesus is all you need until Jesus is all you have." I thank Michael Wells, whose teaching, books and life personified and brought such beautiful simplicity to the Gospel of Jesus Christ—truly John 15 now lives in my actuality, not merely my theology.

Thanks to Chris, my "third" sister, who showed up on the last days of John's life and just bustled around the house doing whatever needed to be done. What a servant.

I thank the ladies of my Wednesday night Bible study (you all know who you are), my "extended family," who listened to my pain and prayed so faithfully for me during the years of John's illness, and who came alongside to help in such practical ways so often. I love you all so much. I appreciate how you stepped in and just did what the body of Christ does when He lives through us—cleaning up my yard before the memorial service, bringing food, keeping everything running smoothly so I would not have to think about anything.

Eunice and Mark, who lavished me with prayer and financial support during the long months waiting for John's retirement to kick in—they were greatly used by God to spare me from the extra burden of financial loss.

I thank the "Broken Vessels" Bible study and prayer women. These faithful friends, mentors, and prayer warriors have, as one of them is fond of expressing, "Stormed the gates of Heaven" for me more often than I deserve. Diane, Sue, Judy, Carole, there are no words for the love, care and encouragement you have been. You all saved me in so many ways in the days after John's death by inviting me out to dinner and lunch and keeping me busy.

To my Sunday School class, the "Fellowship Class," I thank so much for their love, support, encouragement, financial help and most of all their prayers and coming alongside in so many ways. Bob and Marge, Sue and Larry, who offered practical and financial help and organized a work party to get my neglected yard back together.

I remember so fondly those I traveled with to Israel on the Joshua Fund Epicenter tour, and our affectionately named "Bus #2 Church," for we were truly the body of Christ who did Church on that bus, thanks to Amy, our bus captain. Thanks to the entire Bus #2 group who prayed for my husband on the shores of the Galilee—I will never forget that moment.

My Pastor, Chris Inman, who came along late in the process but who formed a bond with me in the middle of my pain and offered help, prayer and encouragement.

I thank my newer writing friend, Nikki, who kept after me to keep writing, and who has taught me so much about the process and about the realm of blogs, web pages, social networking and all of those online mysteries that I never would have figured out on my own.

To Don and Lynda for your generous contribution for the financing of this project. And a special thanks to Westbow Publishing for such prayerful guidance through the process of publishing this book.

There is of course no way I can express my gratefulness to everyone who has contributed in many ways to this book, and so I thank my Lord Jesus; may He pour out His blessings on you all, and may He be glorified by this book.

Introduction

The baby boomers are coming into the aging population. With the aging of the most populous "named" generation comes a health dilemma reported to be of possible epidemic proportions in the next dozen years—namely dementia.

I invite you into my personal journey through the murky maze of walking through the mists of dementia with my beloved spouse. Follow along with me through the heartache of helplessly watching my husband lose his once hilarious personality and quicksilver memory, while slowly fading into a mist where I could not follow.

Experience my wobbly and inadequate faith as God slowly urged me into a surrendered trust even as He led me through long dark passageways of blank discouragement and no-water deserts, finally leading me out into a wide, deep sea of His love, care and compassion. This is a story of growing faith; a story of triumph over failure; a story of God's strength in place of weakness.

In the coming years, many books will offer practical help in maneuvering through the disease of dementia. *Into the Mist,* however, offers a blow-by-blow experience through the excruciating emotional devastation of lives laid waste by the disease. As I learned from hard experience, practical help is necessary; spiritual guidance is essential. How does one handle the guilt when they fear they have failed at caretaking? What to do as you fall helplessly into old memories, or become angry at the person who can no longer control their behavior? Where is God in all of it? What is He planning to unearth in the deep recesses of a broken heart?

I sought for just such a book in vain; thus I wrote this story to offer practical yes, but more importantly, spiritual and emotional healing for the caretaker who is facing this new journey.

Those who will read this book will certainly include all who are facing the demise of a loved one who has a dementia illness. It will also include those who are caretakers, feeling alone with no one to talk to. It was so important to me during John's illness to have someone who had gone before me, had faced the pain and decision-making to assist me along the way, answer my myriad questions or just to tell me that what I was feeling was normal, but I had no one. While there are many helpful books on dementia and caretaking, very few address the spiritual side of the disease. It is my hope that this book addresses that part of the process.

This is the story of my own spiritual journey into the abiding life with Jesus Christ. It is not an ordinary book with a beginning, middle and end. It will not give any formulas for your journey, nor does it have an ending with a typical victorious answer to prayer. Rather, it is an ongoing walk in which I have learned deep, intimate things from my Lord; things such as how much He cares for me and loves me in the middle of overwhelming events in my life; what these events have taught me about myself and my relationships with others, and a host of things I may or may not even be able to relate with words.

In my journey, you will discover deep wrestling with fears, doubts and unbelief which I discovered were so much ingrained in my very being. You will discover that my false concepts of God and my faulty perceptions of how He should behave in any given circumstance were all unraveled, one by one, or as Exodus 23:30 (NKJV) says, "little by little." You may discover for yourself that God cannot be boxed in, He cannot always be figured out, (His ways are "past finding out" Romans 11:33 NKJV.) He will not let up until His strength is perfected in our weakness and He will never forsake us during the process, no matter how many perceived failures we have. You may discover that faith is highly valued by Him, that He may test us to our limits in order to prove to us not whether our faith is real, but rather to prove to us that He is faithful even when we are not ("If we are faithless, He remains faithful; He cannot deny Himself" 2 Timothy 2:13 NKJV.). You may discover that this faith walk proves that true faith happens when we choose to believe even when there is no reason left to believe.

The key to this faith walk is in understanding that God is not merely after an end result; the process is as important as the end. Once one gets hold of this concept—not looking forward to the day when the trial is over, but looking right at the face of Jesus in the middle of the trial, learning from Him everything He wants to teach us, we will be on a journey that will amaze, confound and bring unspeakable joy into our daily life.

In the process of this journey into the deeper walk with Jesus Christ, at the end of it all, I was made aware of a piece of this puzzle one early morning as I sat with Jesus. He gave me a peek behind the veil, of His purpose in our pain. As God brought the children of Israel out from the captivity of Egypt, He instructed them to plunder the enemy, or in the vernacular of our day—take everything valuable you can from them. The plunder were the spoils of war—the victory booty. The children of Israel took from their Egyptian slaveholders all of their gold, silver and every precious and valuable item.

Why would God instruct them to do this? And what did they do with the plunder? They were instructed at a later time to bring all of the plunder—all of the gold, silver and valuable items—and give it for the building of the altar in the temple and the temple utensils used in the Holy place. The plunder was their reward for enduring the years of suffering while in bondage to the Egyptians, and then they brought the reward and offered it back to God.

What is the plunder of my particular trial? I believe that the plunder from my and your trials are the priceless gems that Jesus teaches us in the midst of pain and suffering—those precious times when He surprises us with a Scripture that seemed to be written just for us for just that moment. It is the gem of discovering that within us lie secret places of rebellion, unbelief, pride, fear, anger, bitterness which He is now ready not to condemn us and chastise us for, but rather to dislodge these stubborn issues in order to heal us and set us free from their bondage. This healing is the plunder! He says to us, just as He says to the children of Israel—take it out with you, take the gold, silver and every rare gem that I have redeemed from this secret place within your soul and follow Me.

And what does He want me to do with that plunder? My publisher spoke a word to me as we talked on the phone early in the publishing process which has lodged deep in my soul: He said, "Thank you for not wasting your pain."

Not wasting your pain—not taking the "plunder" and burying it away somewhere. Rather, taking the pain and casting it upon many waters, which will take it to many hurting and wounded souls who can drink deeply of that living water and find freedom in their pain. I so often think of the subject of "living water" as it relates to our relationship with Jesus and as it relates to our day-to-day walk with Him. Living water is rapid, rushing, bubbling water. It is living because the tumbling over rocks and tree roots is what cleans it; it is always fresh. Water that is held in cisterns soon becomes stale and stagnant. As we cast our painful experiences, our wounds, our hidden secret places out into His living water, Jesus cleans it and sends it quickly on to others so that by drinking, they too can be free in Him. He doesn't waste any of it.

By collecting our tears in His bottle, I came to understand that now, when I encounter a woman in the throes of a painful ordeal, He dips into His bottle of my tears and retrieves them. He allows the memory of the pain, the experience of it, to be fresh again, so that I can walk into her pain and offer her the comfort I received from Him, just as He so beautifully illustrates in 2 Corinthians 1:4. If I have kept my tears to myself, hidden them away somewhere because they are just too painful to keep, then I will forget that pain and all of the lessons I learned from it, and I will become a stagnant cistern, or worse, a broken cistern.

With this book, I offer the plunder back to Jesus, so that He can build something beautiful and precious from it, something through which other little birds can be sustained throughout their process of dying to self. I pray that this book will be a place where others can find that rest in Him and His rest upon them.

We are all on a journey of faith, trust, and belief in Jesus Christ. I call on everyone whose journey has reached a rough patch, to press on to the high calling of Christ Jesus; allow Him to redeem the pure from the vile and purify it through His living water with which to quench another pilgrim on their journey.

Jesus is worth it and He is enough.

Prologue
(Fall of 2004)

Alzheimer's disease, thief of time and personality, abducted Ann from the full journey of her life. Each of us Alzheimer's caregivers has experienced this slow but steady diminishment of a loved one; they leave us prematurely, often in the fullness of life while we remain by their side ... The diagnosis of Alzheimer's disease came as a double jolt. Not only did I see the illness threatening Ann's exquisite well-being but also a major part of my own life was about to be ripped away. Soon Ann, lost in space and time, was both gone and still there; well yet very ill; saw yet had no vision; heard yet had little understanding. I was terrified about being too ill-equipped as a caregiver to cope lovingly with such a hideously debilitating illness ... Grappling with the fallout left week by week in the wake of this illness was equally ill-fated, for Alzheimer's savage attacks seemed to threaten the very soul of my loved one. As Charilie, a dear friend, said to me toward the end of Ann's time at home, "It's not like cancer of the belly or the bone, where you have something to fight and someone to fight it with; Alzheimer's is a disease of the soul." (Wayne Ewing, <u>Tears in God's Bottle: Reflections on Alzheimer's Caregiving</u> Whitestone Circle Press, Tucson, AZ, 1999, p. 15)

I cannot remember when John stopped laughing. Try as I might, I cannot recall when it happened, and I so want to remember, for that is the first insight into when this journey began. It was the most remarkable change, because if John was ever known for anything, it was that great, infectious, belly laugh. He could laugh me out of any mood—even when I didn't want to be laughed out of a mood. Though I was sometimes irritated by his attempts to laugh me out of a bad mood, he nevertheless always won out.

I was too busy to notice when he stopped laughing. Was it in 2000, when his mother and my father died within five months of each other? No, we had managed to get away on one of our treasured trips to the ocean that next summer, and I think we laughed, although perhaps not as often. My youngest son and his new wife were in Israel. The terrible intifada had begun there, and I was often lost in thought and worry. John had begun, I think even then, to retreat, showing less care and empathy. But, I didn't notice, except to be hurt by his lack of feeling for my own pain.

It seems as if I can catch glimpses, vapor-like memories, of the beginnings of his diminishment after Jennifer died. My niece, taken so violently from us at the tender age of nineteen, only two short years after my dad died, seemed to add to that huge chasm that had already been left by his death. It felt akin to being in an airplane that had suddenly been ripped open, sucking everyone and everything not bolted down out into the atmosphere. I remember thinking that I should just let go and stop trying to hang on. Somewhere in that darkness, I could hear Jesus telling me that if I did let go, He would hold onto me.

During the interminable four days at the hospital, waiting and crying as she lay in a coma, John never came to my side until the very end. When I called, he would ask if we were still taking our planned trip to the ocean that week. It was not the John I knew who spoke those words, but in my own pain, I could experience only abandonment and anger. How could he be thinking of the trip when Jennifer lay dying? Why was he not with me? Why did he avoid coming to Phoenix?

I think that the accumulation of so many deaths in the span of two years must have played a silent role in our beginning to separate emotionally from each other, but then there was that other thing: the completely changed man I began to witness. Still, we were both busy, he trying to adjust to a new job teaching high school, me teaching two Bible studies. Plus we were selling one house and buying another with Mom. It was a good plan, having Mom live in her own part of the house downstairs. My sister, Linda, bought Mom and Dad's old house, and it turned out to be the best thing for all of us.

But all of the changes seemed to have a cumulative effect on John. He mentioned his frustration at not being able to adjust to the new job, the move, and the new house. He even said he felt depressed, which was very unusual for him. This was in 2002. In the fall of that year, at

Thanksgiving—only two months after moving—we learned that his uncle Ken had died. We made the trip to Maryland shortly after, and it is possible that this is when he stopped laughing as often. Life had become painful, serious—*real*.

Others had noticed; those who didn't see him as often. They remarked to me that John had changed. But in my mind, I felt the problem was with us, with our marriage. Our bickering, sporadic in the past, became more frequent, and our fights took on a menacing tone. He no longer attempted to laugh me out of moods. He was distancing emotionally from me, and I had no idea why. Doing what I always do—blaming myself, trying to change—didn't help at all.

John and I married late. It was my second marriage and his first. I had two sons—Adam and Dane—and while he never pretended he was their father, he took time with them in many of their growing-up needs. He worked on their cars, built model airplanes with them, and tutored them in math and algebra, which I could never have done. Being an only child and with no children of his own, he didn't know how to parent, but I felt he provided a safe place for them to grow up.

I remember him saying once or twice that the best thing he could do for my sons was to love their mother. And he did that. He treated me like a princess. He adored me, fussed over me, and babied me. I was not used to this treatment but found no difficulty growing to love and appreciate it.

Those early years with John were the most wonderful years of my life. I found what I had always longed for: a lifelong companion. I will not try to paint a rosy picture, for there were many problems, too, but these seemed to take a backseat to what was real and good. We had our life with the kids, but we also had our private life, rich with shared love of music, food, restaurants, and road trips.

Oh, the trips! When John could persuade me to break away from my Saturday housecleaning and sweep me away on a day trip, he had a way of making every short trip into a mini-vacation! How many times we traveled down through Skull Valley, always stopping at the little country store for pickled eggs, and then on to Peeple's Valley, where outstretched green fields were punctuated with meandering, towering cottonwoods following some riparian river.

I loved that drive: eating beef jerky and pickled eggs, and listening to jazz on the radio. (I have to smile, thinking that this was not exactly as cosmopolitan as eating aged cheese and sipping fine wine, though we did that as well.) We often ended up in Wickenburg and poked around for hours in the little shops. Other days, we would travel up through Clarkdale and down into Clear Creek, our favorite "Igloo 54" ice chest filled with good cheese, crackers, and beverages. (We had favorite ice chests, which John humorously named "Igloo 54," "Igloo 24," and the "tiny ice chest.")

Wherever we traveled, we had our favorite spots, including our favorite grocery stores, where we bought our favorite foods to take along. These little things—favorite food, favorite stores, favorite restaurants, favorite places—were the tapestry of our lives, all woven together as a much beloved memory quilt. No matter how much time had passed, John never forgot where we had been a year ago, what time, what month, what date, and what we ate. This was true for every event of our lives. These are the things I miss the most.

Our first long trip through Colorado in 1997 was by far the most memorable. We both felt overwhelmed by the state's hugeness. We held our breath over every towering mountain pass, frightened at the narrowness of roads with no guardrails, dropping straight down into five-thousand foot gorges. John perfected his best Irish accent as we drove up and down these mountain passes listening to Celtic music, he mimicking our acquaintance Jim's booming Irish brogue: "Wellllll, Kathy! What do ya think?" We spent three weeks just going where the road took us, stopping wherever we saw a rushing river by the road, and staying the night in the most amazingly beautiful RV parks I can ever remember. And we laughed. We laughed a lot that summer.

The laughter is so important, because I tend to be a more serious person. This made us the perfect match. John freed me from my seriousness, and my seriousness taught him there is more to life than drinking beer and eating good food. We balanced each other in so many ways. If I had it to do over again, I would have laughed more and been far less serious. When John stopped laughing, my world came apart.

Christmas 2003 we took our last extended trip together. We had decided to travel by car across the country to visit his family in Maryland. I can remember this trip by tastes, scents, and feelings. Getting up before dawn, the CRV packed with gifts for the family, the Igloo 54 filled with our favorite travel foods, off we went.

John loved to drive; I think he was at his happiest when we were driving together. On one of our early trips to the ocean, I was content to loll around on the beach while he was anxious to get in the car and drive.

I began calling him "the mad driver," and, thereafter, all of our day trips became "mad drives."

This Christmas, I had plumped up my seat with my "woobies" (my family's name for our down comforters), pillows, books, electronic solitaire—all my comfort things—and snuggled down for what would become one more of those memorable trips to which only John and I could relate. Those little inside jokes and memories made up who we were, and this trip was no different, as we collected new favorites and inside jokes to add to our repertoire. If I close my eyes, I can still experience driving before sunup through the vast Texas landscape, where there are no hills, no mountains, no trees, only sky and endless road. I was bowled over by a sunrise that literally enveloped everything, as though the sunrise *was* everything. We were completely alone in some hidden, sacred place with God. There are no words for such things; "Oh God!" seems sufficient. And so it was for this entire trip.

On the way home, we stopped at Mom's childhood home, now empty and rundown, in Brunswick, Tennessee. I took pictures of the church where, as a little child, she walked forward to receive Christ. The verse on the front of the church read, "Blessed are those who hear the Word of God and keep it," and how true this was in Mom's life. With no training in Christian living and no one who took her to church, she walked along the winding path to this little church on her own. In my inner heart, I am sure that some dear, unknown prayer warrior in that church saw her and began a vigil of prayer, for my mom had indeed heard the Word of God and kept it from that day forward.

In the spring of 2004, my son Adam's marriage unraveled, and his life became a great, sweeping vortex of pain and turmoil into which I found myself swirling in despair. It completely consumed me. My son Dane's life also became a well of torment, as old emotions and unresolved anger began eating away like a cancer at his soul. That summer, after longing to get to the ocean and the fresh salt air, I found no respite in my own soul. I think John and I laughed some, but certainly there was less by then.

How I wish I could remember if we laughed during that summer. I need that memory now, because if we did, it was the last summer that we did. I recall driving up the coast from San Diego to Carlsbad in our rented red Mustang, discovering where the Trader Joe's market was located, always a number-one priority on our trips. I remember walking along the beach at sunset, looking for shells, as we always did, and sitting on a rock to watch the sun go down over the ocean. Those memories are like the collection of shells we have from over the years—little bits and pieces of the life we lived together.

In the summer of 2004, John's distancing became more apparent. We were unhappy, always at odds over something. It seemed the whole world was in turmoil. Hurricanes were worse than any on record and doing bizarre things—heading out to sea and then suddenly making U-turns and crossing their own paths, heading back to land to devastate everything in their paths. They marched across the Atlantic one after the other—Charley, Frances, Gaston, Ivan, Jeanne, Karl, Lisa, all category three and up. Ivan barely missed New Orleans and then traveled on land up to New York and back into the Atlantic, turning around and coming back to South Florida, where it hit the Gulf, re-formed, and headed toward New Orleans, petering out before doing any damage. Some scientists have dubbed certain wind forces as the "finger of God," and it appeared to be so that summer.

Then there were the earthquakes, everywhere it seemed. A 7.2 in Japan; several in California, called a "swarm"; several in Indonesia, culminating in December of 2004 with the 9.2 off the coast of Indonesia and the devastating tsunami. Newspaper headlines dubbed these of "biblical proportion."

It was a turbulent year; our presidential elections were turbulent and then the death of Arab leader Yasser Arafat. Other key leaders were being elected or stepping down in key hot points around the world. The landscape of the world seemed to be experiencing a polar shift. There were polar shifts at the most personal level and at the most extreme world levels.

CHAPTER ONE

Out of the Depths I Have Cried

(Journal entry 10/13/04)

Out of the depths I have cried to You, O LORD; Lord, hear my voice! Let Your ears be attentive To the voice of my supplications. If You, LORD, should mark iniquities, O Lord, who could stand? But there is forgiveness with You, That You may be feared. I wait for the LORD, my soul waits, And in His word I do hope. (Psalm 130:1–5 NKJV)

In the midst of this turbulence, the Lord sent a gift to me. In November, a speaker named Michael Wells spoke at our church, and his message struck my heart so profoundly that I can only say my faith walk took a dramatic turn after hearing him. The message from John 15 was simple yet profound: being so at one with Jesus that no matter what is going on in life, because Jesus abides in us and we in Him, we can live with only His life flowing through us. This means that in the turbulence, Jesus is never overwhelmed; therefore, I need not be overwhelmed. This message would prove to be a saving grace for all that was coming, and I will be forever grateful to God for bringing it to me at this time.

On November 9, 2004, Jim, John's principal, called. John had blacked out at his desk, and they were taking him to the ER. I met them there and listened in disbelief as John recounted for the doctor that he had these blackouts several times in the past few months, one time waking up on the floor of our living room while I was gone. As was now typical of our drifting apart, this was one more instance where I felt he had left me out of

1

his life. This distancing had been progressing over the past year or so, and it hurt me that something as serious as this had been kept from me.

They admitted him, attached heart monitors, and scheduled him for an MRI of his brain and other tests. That first day in the hospital room, he once again began to black out and pushed the nurse's button. They came in with the printout from the monitor, which showed that his heart had apparently stopped beating for five seconds. The nurses were encouraged, however, as this gave them a diagnosis. After consulting with the cardiologist, they scheduled him for a pacemaker and canceled the MRI.

After the pacemaker surgery, John's entire personality began to change. First, he was what I can only describe as euphoric, very high almost and full of restless energy. At the same time, he began to lose his memory. I noticed it when putting photos into my picture albums. He walked by and saw a photo of an old family friend and asked who she was. John never forgot a face or a name. When I seemed surprised and told him, he later told me that he had no recollection of her or her connection to us. This would begin the long, painful journey into the mist of dementia.

CHAPTER TWO

He Has Known Your Wanderings Through This Great Wilderness

(Journal entry 11/30/04)

This thing, I cannot describe it, descends on me. I will be okay, and suddenly this darkness descends. It just takes over my emotions. Usually it relates to something John says or does … This happened Wednesday before Thanksgiving, it happened again the day after, when John seemed to come under it and screamed at me. I am in a place of very deep training from the Lord. He is pruning and putting to death many things. It is painful, even frightening, but necessary.

His temper seemed to be growing more menacing. I would become angry at him because he was so distant and unfeeling, and I didn't know what was happening. By December of 2004, the abiding life teachings had begun to slowly weave their way into my very being. I wrote in December,

> My heart is full this morning, Lord. The city is blanketed in white. Your presence is near and I am full of thanksgiving to You for the work You are doing in the midst of the trials. I love You so much. The first passage of Scripture I read as I closed my journal seems so appropriate: "For the LORD your God has blessed you in all that you have done; He has known your wanderings through this great wilderness.

These forty years the LORD your God has been with you;
you have not lacked a thing." (Deuteronomy 2:7 NASB)

I went on to thank Him for the painful trials of the past year, for the wonderful verses He spoke to my heart in the midst of these trials, and for His presence. I would need all of it, every tiny bit, of what God was teaching me to prepare me for the year ahead.

I now began to notice something new with John: a nervous pacing, impatience, as though he was anticipating going somewhere and anxious for me to get ready. He would follow me around, stand watching me, and then pace some more. He became obsessed with little inconsequential details, fussing over them, worrying; this was yet another unfamiliar character trait. I wish I could say that I was instantly and spontaneously kind and loving when I began to notice these changes. But, so much distance and separation had taken place already in our relationship, together with all the peripheral distractions of our lives, that I failed to see this was all a part of what was happening in his brain. I only became irritated with him, and when I got irritated, he would become defensive and angry. There seemed to be constant friction.

One day after work, he decided to drive all the way to Phoenix just to get color cartridges for the printer. I should have seen these warning signs, but John had always been a spontaneous person and enjoyed driving long distances. Still, I knew this time it was out of the ordinary. He also became more antisocial toward my family and others, to the point of being downright rude many times. I was concerned but still felt it was a problem that had grown in our relationship.

He was constantly reminiscing about his old memories, old friends, and family. He called his family more often, as well as friends from his past, whom he hadn't seen or heard from in years. It was as if he were pining for his old life and old memories. He had distanced himself from me more during this time and wanted to return to his past. In retrospect, I can see it was the older memories that he recalled and were now more familiar to him. The more recent memories were patchy and full of holes. It was somehow more comforting to him to have memories that were not filled with holes.

"He heals the brokenhearted, And binds up their wounds" (Psalm 147:3 NASB).

During this time, a peculiar thing happened. I had been down in the dumps over not being able to communicate with John. Because of the terrible oppression hanging over our house, I frequently awoke in the middle of the night and went into my prayer closet to read my Bible and pray. I often sat alone, crying as I read. I had begun to blame myself for John's bizarre behavior, as John himself seemed to believe he was fine and that all the problems were with me. I wonder how many dementia caretakers can relate to this almost surreal thought: *Maybe it is me! Maybe I am the one losing touch with reality.*

I woke late one night after a disturbing dream and went into my prayer room to read some Scripture and talk to Jesus. Reading Proverbs 31, I felt convicted that I had not been to John what he needed, and I felt so guilty at my failures as a wife. John continuously told me that I was making up his symptoms, and I'm sure this contributed to my feelings of failure. A few days later, my sister Pat's friend in Tucson, Betty (who had no way of knowing anything about my dilemma as we had never met or talked), called Pat to tell her that on that same night, she had awoke in the middle of the night and was urged to go into another room to pray. This was not something she normally experienced, so she asked the Lord for what she was to pray. She picked up the prayer book Pat and I had written, saw my name, and decided to pray for me. What she heard from the Lord and what she told Pat the next day was, "Tell Kathy that Jesus sees her as the Proverbs 31 woman." She also had been led to pray, "No weapon that is formed against you shall prevail." When Pat shared this with me, my heart nearly burst with joy. Jesus had spoken to me through a complete stranger. He was not disappointed with me, and He was there. It set the stage for an intimate relationship with Him that would supersede everything else in life at that time.

For God alone my soul awaits in silence. (Psalm 62:1)

All I could write about was my journey. John's mind refused to allow him to experience what was happening. His absence in the process proved to be almost as difficult for me as the disease itself, because I was left to face it alone. It was not a shared experience as so many of our experiences had been. We shared our love of so many things. We shared the difficulty of raising the kids. We shared financial trials and hardships, the deaths of our parents.

It is hard now to define the degree of adjustment to this new experience, going through it together but so alone. I could write volumes just on the struggle of getting him to see a doctor. God intervened when he had another fainting episode a few months after the pacemaker, and he happened to tell my sister Linda and niece Kim. (He didn't tell me, of course; for some unknown reason I was no longer his partner in these things.) They are nurses, and they urged him to go to the doctor and have a CT scan. He finally consented, and the CT showed he had a colloid cyst in his third ventricle. This, as it turns out, was an incidental finding, but God used it to get us moving toward a more intense neurological search for answers.

CHAPTER THREE

A Haze of Confusion and Flare-Ups

(Journal Entry 2/13/05)

The deep places God has taken me these past few months are amazing to me. He is revealing things that have been hidden in the secret chambers of my heart—places I retreat to when wounded by John, or when a new crisis arises with one of the kids—that I now know have been idols. As each idol is revealed, I exchange it for Jesus. I put it under the blood and trust that it is no longer mine and I can no longer retrieve it and worship it. This process has been the most excruciatingly painful, yet at the same time the most delightful, than any I have known in a long while.

Throughout the spring of 2005, our lives became a haze of confusion and flare-ups. John was becoming more distant to me and rude to our friends and family. The couples' Bible study had to be moved from our house to another, because it caused such anxiousness and irritability in him. We were watching Michael Wells's videos on the abiding life, but John was completely uninterested. He sat with a stony face, not communicating with anyone. He seemed insecure and unsure of himself but, at the same time, struggling to maintain control over his own affairs and life. He was greatly agitated by the smallest things, such as loud noises. People talking or laughing too loudly caused him to become irritated.

In my mind, the battle still appeared to be related to problems in our relationship; more and more I sensed that he was leaving me. From the Abiding Life teaching, I felt I was taking a new path in my relationship with John. God was fine-tuning something very deep inside, where He was breaking down my old emotional feelings for John, even my very love for him, so He could replace it with His own love. I wish I could report that I eased into this transition with grace, but it was more like a tearing away of literal flesh, and it was intense and painful.

I began making a simple exchange: "I exchange this feeling of rejection I am experiencing right now, Lord, for Your own love and mercy." Where I had always in my past walk of faith dug into the deeper truths of God's word, gleaning out the unseen nuggets to teach to others, I had returned to the very simple walk of childlike faith. I was being trained in love, a love that is supernatural from God. It was important that my own natural love be exchanged, as my love gets its back up when offended. It needs constant reassurance that it is loved in return; it is selfish.

In the meantime, the march of family upheavals continued unabated, and I was again caught up in the peripheral side eddies of the day-to-day busyness.

The summer of 2005 was a wasteland of emotional devastation.

I had finally reached such a low point that I asked to have lunch with Diane, who, with her husband Guy, had invited Michael Wells to our church the previous fall. They had been teaching the Abiding Life material, and I had begun attending their Sunday school class. When I met Diane for lunch, everything spilled out, and together we shared our experiences of coming to the end of ourselves and of the deeper walk with the Lord. Over lunch that day, we liberally salted our salads with our tears. This would become an enduring friendship, sent from the hand of God. He spoke to me in many ways that day; I had so much to learn about this new journey.

The following week, John seemed to be his old self. These were the confusing times, the days when his old self broke through and the ordeal appeared to be over at last. But without warning, it would reappear, plunging me into what I came to call "the pit." For me, that pit would come at unexpected times, the times I let down my guard—usually when I began to feel that things were going to be normal again. It was then a sudden shift would occur.

These shifts were difficult to define. It was not so much that they were related to a definite event, rather more like a shift in an unseen dimension, where things around me looked the same but there was the sense they were off kilter, out of balance somehow. During one of those shifts into seeming normalcy, we traded our Minnie Winnie for a smaller, sleeker,

RV. We loved it, and it promised to be the beginning of new and exciting travel adventures.

We excitedly looked forward to our first trip in the new RV—Big Lake in the White Mountains, one of our favorite places. Our favorite campground was in Greer, where we had camped several times, and, of course, we had our favorite restaurant, our favorite spot by the reservoirs, and our favorite mad drives. Getting up into the cool mountain air was a balm to my soul after a long, difficult winter. Living in the sun-parched drought of the southwest, this part of eastern Arizona always seemed to have defied the drought. No matter what time of summer we visited, we were always blessed by soft afternoon showers, which were like liquid gold to us.

CHAPTER FOUR

Big Lake: The Big Event

(Journal Entry June 2005)

Finally, we got away on Wednesday. Oh! What bliss to drive out of town! But I had not been sleeping, had only slept maybe three hours Tuesday night and even on the trip I had trouble sleeping. There is something—a sense of dread—that I fight every night. It takes hours to get my focus back on the Lord.

At Big Lake we settled in to our campsite. The early green was still on the trees—that almost fluorescent glow that the early leaves cast—a soft green mist under the canopy of tall aspens and pines. The stress of the past several months began to melt off, as I prepared for several days of driving around with John, sitting in my camping rocker, and reading some new books.

On the drive to Big Lake, we passed a new pull-off viewpoint, and John remarked it hadn't been there when we were there last. I reminded him that it was still under construction at that time and now was finished. We agreed to stop and look out over the vast valley below when we came back through the next day, which we did. Standing at the overlook, we talked about the nice improvements and the addition of picnic areas. We went on to do some shopping in Springerville. As we always did on our trips, we reminisced about all the previous trips, what we did, what we bought. This day was no exception, and John seemed to recall the places we had visited. We went to Safeway and the Dollar Store and then back to the lake. It was a good day; we were getting along and feeling good.

The next day we drove to Greer. It was here that this new enemy invaded our retreat. John's mood shifted. He seemed confused, anxious, nervous. He kept pointing out that everything in Greer had changed; he didn't recognize things he had readily known in the past. He couldn't remember the campground where we had stayed before or the restaurant we loved. He vaguely remembered the reservoirs where we had taken so many lovely walks in the past, but clearly, something was not right.

Driving to our favorite grassy meadow on the Little Colorado River, his mood became detached, uninterested, and he kept repeating over and over that everything had changed. He was anxious to get going, not wanting to walk around like we normally did. We drove back to the reservoirs to fix lunch, but he was not interested in getting out of the van and walking along the water's edge, as we loved to do. We ate a hurried lunch and headed back to our campsite.

Coming out of the area of the reservoirs, he could not remember which way to turn and insisted on going the wrong direction, back toward Greer. I was now alarmed and frightened. John had never lost his way, not ever. Now he seemed unsure of everything and unable to find his way back to the road. He had forgotten that we had just passed the reservoirs and commented that he thought we might have been there before.

Now my mind was racing. What was going on? What was happening to my husband? This was not a problem with our relationship, as I had thought. There was something terribly, terribly wrong with John. I expressed my alarm and fear to him, but he only retaliated in anger. I cried all the way back to camp, yet he seemed not to notice me at all. It rained off and on all night, a soft cadence on the roof of the van. I lay awake, crying out to God.

The next morning, John was fearful and anxious because of the rain and obviously fearful of a storm that was coming. He wanted to pack up and go home early. I encouraged him that it was just a summer storm and we would be fine. We took a walk around the campground, but it was not the easy, leisurely walks we had always known. It was hurried and fretful. From that time, everything became hurried and fretful.

I continued to encourage him to relax and stay; I even talked him into going back into Springerville to pick up something he had expressed interest in two days ago. Driving past the lookout point, he pulled in and began the identical conversation we had two days ago, commenting that they must have made all the changes since we were there two years ago. He seemed not to remember that we had discussed that before. Arriving in Springerville, he couldn't remember where True Value was, even though we had been there two days ago. He saw Safeway and the Dollar Store and said, "We went there before, didn't we? Or maybe not." Again, I sat, watching and listening to him, and a cold fear began to settle over me. When he went in to True Value, I stayed in the van and called Linda, because I now was genuinely frightened. I was back in that pit, crying and scared.

When John got back in the van and saw that I was crying, he asked me what was wrong. I tried to tell him how scared I was at what was happening to him, but he only became angry and defensive, shouting at me to just shut up. The overwhelming realization that my husband might be seriously ill, and that he was not going to let me help him, hit me hard. He only accused me of making it up, blowing it out of proportion.

Now the battle was on in earnest—a battle against some unseen force that had invaded my husband. We went back to the campsite, and he began feverishly packing up to leave, desperate to get out of there before the storm came. Oblivious to my presence, he fixated on the storm. He seemed confused about why I was crying, but angry when I tried to explain what I could see happening to him. I realized that if my husband were ill, I would be expected to watch from the sidelines, not allowed to help, and this was unimaginable to me. I was his helpmate, I was there in sickness and health, but he was pushing me out, and there would be nothing I could do to stop this train that was careening out of control.

The drive back home was endless. He drove too fast around the mountain curves, bolting for home, me crying in the back. At home, he was angry, confused, shouting. And then he became violent.

For people going through this ordeal with dementia, the confusion is staggering. Your mind refuses to process it; it clutches desperately to what was normal. My beloved husband was no longer there; he was gone. Someone else had moved into his body, and I did not know this man. This thing had robbed us of our special memories together. It robbed us of affection and tenderness. It robbed us of conversation. I was afraid, angry, and alone, and I had no idea what to do. I began a fragmented sort of grieving, grieving the death of someone who was familiar and dear to me, but trying to live with this stranger who had moved into my home, invaded my husband's body. How can you grieve the loss of someone when he is still there, still trying to control his life?

CHAPTER FIVE

The Little Birds: Do You Not Believe?

(Journal Entry 6/29/05)

Lord Jesus, my Rock, my Tower, my Refuge, You know all these things and only You can reveal, expose, and destroy these works of darkness that have taken such hold on us. I will hide in You until these calamities be overpast. (Isaiah 26:20)

In the little book *They Found the Secret*, the story of Walter L. Wilson stirred my heart. I found his prayer to strike such a chord in me that I read it for myself:

I prayed this with the deepest part of myself. I believed that Jesus was about to do some deep changing of my heart and I must pay attention now to every detail of what He would teach me. Yet, there still remained this nagging sense that this was a marital problem; somehow this was my fault, and I could fix it. It would be a long while before Jesus would be able to penetrate that relentless self-examination and self-blame and convince me that He was not blaming me. Instead, He was there to encourage and comfort me.

My Lord, I have mistreated You all my Christian life. I have treated You like a servant. When I wanted You I called for You; when I was about to engage in some work I beckoned You to come and help me perform my task. I have kept You in the place of a servant. I have sought to use You only as a willing servant to help me in my self-appointed and chosen work. I shall do so no more. Just now I give You this body of mine; from my head to my feet, I give it to You. I give You my hands, my limbs, my eyes and lips, my brain; all that I am within and without, I hand over to You for You to live in it the life that You please. You may send this body to Africa, or lay it on a sick bed with cancer. You may blind the eyes, or send me with Your message to Tibet. You may take this body to the Eskimos, or send it to a hospital with pneumonia. It is Your body from this moment on. Help Yourself to it. Thank You, my Lord. I believe You have accepted it for in Romans twelve and one you said "acceptable unto God." Thank You again, my Lord, for taking me. We now belong to each other. (Edman, Raymond V., *They Found The Secret.* Grand Rapids, MI: Zondervan Corp., 1960, 1984, p. 154)

In my times of pain and darkness, I retreated to my little room, where I prayed and cried it all out to Jesus, many times in the still of a long and sleepless night. During one such time, I asked Him what I should do, what I could do. Reading from the Word, I found:

But about midnight Paul and Silas were praying and singing hymns of praise to God, and the prisoners were listening to them; and suddenly there came a great earthquake, so that the foundations of the prison house were shaken; and immediately all the doors were opened, and everyone's chains were unfastened. (Acts 16:25, 26 NASB)

I distinctly heard Him say, "I want you to pray and sing hymns of praise; that is all. I will be responsible for others who are listening and watching and I will cause an earthquake in the spiritual realm and I will loose the chains." From this point on, this truth returned again and again. I tried putting on Christian music and letting it play while I worked around the house, but that did not seem to be what He meant.

Later, after I had shared this with my daughter-in-law, Tasha, she tried to listen to her music and finally realized that Jesus wanted her to sing to Him. So, she got out her hymnbook and started singing old hymns. She related that her little children came from all over the house to sit quietly and snuggle while she sang. This struck me so deeply that I dug out all the hymns I could find and began my mornings singing to Jesus. I now saw

Him in the simplest things. My mind is not simple, it never shuts down, but now I was being asked to stop everything, stop trying to figure it all out, and just do what He asked. What He seemed to be asking was almost too easy for me. I wondered at what point in my Christian walk I had made faith so much more complicated than Jesus had ever intended it to be.

While Jesus was doing this new work in me, however, I continued to battle with the conflicting and confusing thoughts that remained for many months to come. So often I felt that God was expecting something from me, but I kept letting Him down. I wanted to go through this trial with grace, but my pain got in the way. What could I do with all of this pain?

In July, John took a trip to Maryland for three weeks to visit his family. I was thankful for the reprieve. I needed this time alone to regroup, be alone with the Lord. My family gathered closely around me during this time, and I gained a new appreciation for my grown sons, so strong and with such godly counsel, and for my close personal family.

While John was gone, I felt led to contact the neurologist at Barrow Neurological Institute in Phoenix, whom we had seen in May for the colloid cyst. I explained to her all of John's new symptoms and behavior changes, which alarmed her greatly. She wanted to see him right away. Because he was out of town, she scheduled him with a cognitive specialist for the first week after he returned.

When John came home, he told me of a verse he had read while he was away: "Remember ye not the former things, neither consider the things of old" (Isaiah 43:18 KJV). The next Sunday, sitting in church together, the sermon seemed directed toward us, and we held hands tightly. I heard Jesus whisper in my ear, "Behold, I do a new thing." I had no idea what this might mean, so I tucked it away. In Sunday school a few weeks later, John related the Isaiah 43:18 passage to our Sunday school class, and I looked it up as the lesson continued. Amazingly, the very next verse—"'Behold, I will do a new thing; now it shall spring forth; shall ye not know it? I will even make a way in the wilderness, and rivers in the desert'"—was the same one I had heard whispered in my ear. What could this mean, Lord? I had no idea.

On the day of the appointment with the cognitive specialist, John seemed confused and unable to find his way to the office, which we had visited a few months before. He seemed defiant, asking everyone except me how to get to the doctor's building. In my mind, I saw it as a stubborn refusal to allow me to be involved in any of this, even rejecting my attempts to give the right directions. Many times over the next year this scene would be repeated, and each time, instead of seeing that this was part of this dreaded disease, I only felt more rejected and relegated to the sidelines. How was I going to face this long ordeal that awaited us in the now unknown, unchartered territory we were embarking upon if I could not even give my husband simple directions to the doctor when he got lost?

The doctor gave him some simple cognitive tests and then scheduled him for neuropsychiatric evaluation. We waited over a month to see this next doctor, and this began the long process of scheduling for test after test, doctor after doctor, sometimes with a month or more between appointments. I had no idea what to expect with each doctor, no idea what to expect with each test. The doctors seemed to associate with the disease more than with us, and many times, I would break down in the office while trying to explain what was going on with my husband.

John sat emotionless, as the doctors asked me to explain how things were from my perspective. I felt as though I were tattling on my husband right in front of him. He, of course, denied there was anything wrong, which made it even more difficult. This ravaged my emotions. Only those who have been through the process of knowing there is something terribly wrong with their loved one and then waiting for a doctor to give them some insight, some tiny thread of a diagnosis, and having that hope disappointed time and again can truly understand what it is like, what it does to you emotionally.

The months between appointments and tests only intensified this roller coaster, as John would be one day seemingly normal and the next day completely changed. Well-meaning friends tried to encourage me by telling me they thought he was fine, but this only compounded my pain, because I felt so alone, as though I were the only one who thought there was something wrong. I often lay awake nights, believing that it was really me, that I was only imagining it. Worse, that I was putting my husband through this terrible ordeal and actually creating his problems. The enemy of our souls knows, indeed, where our weak points are, and he played with mine with all the skill of a symphony conductor.

A few days after this appointment, we went to White Horse Lake and parked our RV on a beautiful campsite by the lake, where we truly relaxed and unwound for the first time all summer. John seemed to be able to rest; he wasn't pacing and restless to leave. It was a perfect reprieve for both of us. An eagle flew every day to the same overarching limb on a tall Ponderosa pine tree, and I felt this was a personal message to me from God. I was beginning to see His hand reaching down, nearly visible in these little, comforting ways, as if to reassure me that He was there and would go through this with us.

While John was in Maryland, I visited a pastor and his wife, Richard and Trudy, whom Diane had recommended to me earlier. As we talked, I expressed my fear of the future, especially the financial future. Richard asked me, "If God takes care of the little birds, and He tells you that you are of much more value to Him than they are, do you believe Him?"

I broke down and cried. I had always thought I believed that, but in reality, I believed it only with my mind. It had never penetrated my heart.

This promise would return to me again and again in innumerable ways over the next months. It was a very personal message to me from God as John and I loved birds—loved watching them out our window at home and whenever we traveled. Sometime during the past couple of years, I had driven alone to sit beside a local lake to pray, when suddenly, an eagle flew very low, near to my car window, so near I could see his eyes and magnificent white head. I recalled Isaiah 40:31: "Those who wait for the LORD will gain new strength; They will mount up with wings like eagles, They will run and not get tired, They will walk and not become weary" (NASB).

CHAPTER SIX

Will You Lay Down Your Life?

(Journal Entry 8/15/05)

I felt like I had let Jesus down too many times, getting angry at John when I should have shown compassion, feeling sorry for myself and going back to the pit. I couldn't get hold of this thing before it got out of control and I would never get it right. I went to that dark place—back to square one; pain spilling out all over the place. I left off even trying to get hold of it and back to that place of peace. I just left it all. I determined I could do nothing at all. Everything I try—even offering it as a forsaken idol to Jesus did not remove it from my mind and heart—it is always resurrected by some little trigger. I always succumb to it and sink into it.

On the morning of August 25, I had decided not to read anymore, not to try anymore. I gave it all up. For some reason, however, I picked up my Oswald Chambers devotional book and read the devotion for that day:

> I have called you friends (John 15:15). The final aim of self-sacrifice is to lay down your life for your Friend. (Chambers, Oswald. *My Utmost For His Highest*, Grand Rapids, MI: Discovery House Publishers, 1963, p. 238)

Jesus spoke audibly to my heart, "Will you lay it all down for Me?" I cried, "Yes." He knew my heart; He knew I wanted to do this; I must do this. Although it was only a few minutes, a profound transaction took place between Jesus and I in that quiet early morning watch.

Going into my living room, I turned on a Christian TV station, and there was Beth Moore, camera up close, tears streaming down her cheeks, as she told of her own personal dark place and her struggle to escape the bondage of it. I listened in awe, as she quoted the passage from Acts 16:25–26, the same passage Jesus had given to me two days before. She spoke of the power she felt when her own chains were broken, as it was she herself who was in bondage, and it was her own chains Jesus loosened. I felt, as she was speaking, the presence of Christ right there with me, pressing this truth into me: *He is doing this! He is going to set me free from all this pain, I am only to sing and pray.* I began to feel shackles coming off, as I knew He would do it for me and through me. I had proven I couldn't do it. I couldn't even do the simple act of laying it down; He had to do it all. He had to do it all.

Soon after this, as John and I were driving somewhere, he—as he often had begun to do—mentioned that he didn't think he needed to see any more doctors, and again, he accused me of making up all of this. This was one of those hot buttons for me, but this time, I turned my face away, looked out my window, and simply said in my heart, *Thank You, Jesus, that You will field this one for me.* And the anger was instantly gone.

Such a simple truth; such a profound thing I was learning: Jesus in me will do it all. He will take the insults and the pain. I need only to turn to Him immediately, and release it to Him. How often He would prove this to me from then on. *Jesus will field it; He will run interference between the dark place of my thoughts and me. This is all new to me. One step at a time, Lord, one step at a time.*

In the days to come, I would need this more than I ever knew, because it is the nature of this disease that the person has no idea what they may be saying or doing. Nor do they have any concept of the impact of their behavior on others. They may say hurtful things, especially to the ones closest to them, and then show absolutely no remorse for their words and even seem confused at the reaction of hurt.

CHAPTER SEVEN

New Revelation of Old Truth: We Are Free to Fail

(Journal Entry 9/7/05)

"We are free to fail because God is a God of compassion ... The only way out of failure is faith. We do not wallow in self-pity and guilt, but we allow failure to bring us to a place of true dependence ... As we begin to live out our life in Christ, experiencing the deeper walk that abiding in Him yields, the works of the enemy correspondingly intensify. No longer will he use the obvious and overt to turn us away from Christ, but rather sly new attacks which consist of well-placed lies to thwart the production of so much fruit ... [W]e will know if we have truly hit on the answer to defeat by how hard the enemy will work in the coming weeks to take them out of the abiding life. I have frequently watched him unleash everything at his disposal to drive a brother or sister back to the state of saving self, denying the cross and unbelief in order to keep that one from abiding in the truth. Basically we know that we are moving in the right direction if things get worse before they get better. (Wells, Michael. *Sidetracked in the Wilderness.* Littleton, CO: Abiding Life Press,1991, pp. 170, 171, 173)

As the tension continued to mount with John, the confusion over whether what was happening to us was because of some unknown brain disease, or if he had simply stopped caring, continued to plague my every thought. His distancing from me, his cruel remarks, and lack of empathy mounted daily, causing me to slink away to cry or rise up to retaliate. Michael Wells writes,

> The confusion over where the true battle is: Many continue to respond to the negative statements of their mates, believing that logic and reason will prevail. They believe that their present problem is due to misunderstanding or wrong thinking, and if only they can appeal to reason and make a good case for their side of the argument, then there will be agreement and harmony. (Ibid., p. 181)

He goes on to speak of that total surrender, and again, the Lord showed me the things I had not surrendered. I had not surrendered my rights or my strong desire to be valued, appreciated, and needed by my husband. Because he would not give me these, I would not surrender. Wells continues:

> The couples in this deception, each holding on to his or her right to be in control, lying in bed, refusing to touch each other and declining to communicate, forfeit the abundant life. They have pain and loss because they do not have total surrender. The kind of forgiveness, love, submission, and respect ... which the Lord requires of us will never come if based on their actions. The Lord makes such demands on the basis of how He has treated us, not how others have acted. As we give up all, we too, will find great joy, not pain and loss. Do not allow the enemy to have this foothold; right now with your mouth, give up that one thing which is allowing him to steal joy that is rightfully yours. (Ibid., p. 182)

So, I surrendered—again. Each time, it felt as if one more chain was loosed. How many of these chains were there? How long would this take? Though what was happening to us was because of this unknown brain disease, Jesus needed to have me in such a place of submission to Him that no matter what happened my reactions would be filtered only through Him, not through my own filter of pain and rejection. At the time, I had no idea why this was happening, but I knew it was a necessary part of this whole process. If John had been diagnosed with cancer, something we could identify and face together, there might not have been this ongoing conflict within my soul: the conflict of whether what was happening was due to marriage problems or because of the symptoms he was exhibiting. So far, no one had told me he had any kind of brain disease, so I was constantly guessing and second-guessing.

As had become normal, things took another turn. John acted almost euphoric again, restless, pacing constantly, looking out the windows and commenting how beautiful everything was. Driving up Rosser Street one day, he stopped the car in the middle of the road to look out over his now favorite scene of the San Francisco Peaks off in the distance. He commented over and over, "Amazing," or, "Look at that. Isn't it beautiful?"

His memory seemed worse; he had forgotten key things we used to do, even recent things we had done together. He told me he believed the colloid cyst had burst after he had bumped his head and was now gone. If I disagreed with him or argued with him on anything, he would become intensely angry and tell me to shut up. Anger just beneath the surface erupted inappropriately.

Again, just as I would begin to feel overwhelmed and was about to give up, Jesus sent me the same message from a different messenger. This time, it was a woman speaker who said, "'Run to Jesus. Run to Him first. Praise and worship confuses the enemy'" (2 Chronicles 20:21). There it was again—praise and singing.

CHAPTER EIGHT

Tearing Down Old Foundations

(Journal Entry 10/05)

Jesus, You have brought down this house of cards. It is all lying here in a rubble. You have begun a good work here, a work the enemy would dearly love to destroy before it ever gets off the ground. You allowed me to see how much I still need you to do it all. There is yet more to tear down of all these things. Please finish what You have begun for Your name's sake. Amen.

Our twentieth anniversary turned into a perfectly blessed time. We took the RV and went to a shady park in Camp Verde, near Clear Creek, and parked under a graceful Arizona sycamore tree, which filled to the brim every afternoon with chattering birds and a cacophony of music. Nothing invaded our time here. We relaxed and enjoyed each other as if nothing had ever happened. On our anniversary, we decided to have dinner in Strawberry, where we had spent the first night of our honeymoon twenty years before. The Strawberry Lodge never changes, never tries to keep up with the pretentiousness or the overdone quaintness of most little mountain towns. Thus, we both were transported back in time to those young and so in love times. Another precious memory to add to the memory box in my mind.

On November 4, 2005, John had his doctor's appointment with the neuropsychologist, who gave him a series of cognitive tests. He asked me many questions, too. Our answers about how John was doing were completely opposite, however, and I had the same sinking feeling in the pit of my stomach that I was making it up and John was fine. He kept insisting that he was fine, and he often did seem fine. So, it must be me.

After three hours of testing, the doctor called me back in. He said that while John scored very well on many of the tests, the tests in the frontal lobe areas of his brain showed a lower than normal score, and he concluded there was frontal lobe diminishing. Though John heard this for himself, he seemed not to hear at all. He continued to insist that he was fine; he may have some memory problems, but no one can be expected to remember everything.

After a few days of this, I finally came apart. The stress of pretending that everything was fine so John would feel fine became extremely difficult. I cried out to him that I couldn't keep carrying this all alone, that we needed to face this together. Something finally broke through at that moment, as he came to me, hugged me, and told me that he knew there was something wrong and that he was scared. He apologized for accusing me of making it up. A tremendous weight was lifted from me. I told him I was scared, too, but I loved him and would be there for him no matter what. I held onto this moment, because he soon returned to his denials and accusations.

I was so emotional during those days. I realized that I was in mourning for John. In our make-believe lives, we talked only about the weather, the cat, and what to have for dinner. He seemed to fixate on where the cat was, looking for him, asking if I had seen him.

On December 6, we met again with the neurologist at Barrow, and after examining the results from the psych test, he stated that John was possibly suffering from something called mild cognitive impairment (MCI), or frontotemporal dementia. He explained there was a loss of executive functioning, which meant that John had difficulty making judgments, including decision making, processing information, and abstract thinking. When John heard "mild," he seemed relieved, and he reiterated that he had only mild memory loss.

Still not fully understanding all that the doctor was telling us, I began to cry and told the doctor that John did not believe there was anything wrong with him and that no matter how bad it was, he refused to believe me.

The doctor explained that because of the nature of this disease, John would not know or understand that he is experiencing these behavioral changes—and that I wouldn't be able to talk him into believing it.

At last I had confirmation that what I had been experiencing was real, not a figment of my imagination. John was not doing these things on purpose: he had no control over it. We made an appointment to see a cognitive specialist on December 27 and returned home.

After John went to bed, I researched MCI and frontotemporal dementia, and my heart sank. It was incurable, degenerative, rapidly accelerating, and would likely progress to Alzheimer's-type symptoms. The life span is normally between two and ten years. And sometimes, it reverses. I decided, that will be my prayer.

CHAPTER NINE

From Shock to Blank Grief

(Journal Entry 12/10/05)

We were told he has mild cognitive impairment, which is very serious. Since then, I have gone from shock to almost detachment to blank grief.

My sister, Pat, visited us and shared that she was also experiencing what we now called our "dark night of the soul." It was difficult for any of us to get into the Christmas spirit, but we all went to the Acker music festival downtown, something we had always loved to do. This local event in Prescott is a precious time of meeting with old friends, dressing in festive clothes, and bundling up to walk around the courthouse square to listen to the music groups playing in each store. We went early to eat and then off to enjoy the festivities. Afterward, John and I drove around to look at the lights.

John and I had tickets to our church musical the next evening. My sisters and I had shopped in the afternoon and when I returned home, he had been taking a nap and seemed disoriented. I began to tell him about my day and when I mentioned Pat, he asked, "Pat? Your sister Pat? Is she here? How long has she been up here?" We had been together all week, but he remembered none of it. I was completely stunned. This was the worst memory lapse yet. I wanted to stay home and cry, I was so overwhelmed, but I couldn't. How disconcerting it is that when we go through the darkest times in life, there is the sense that all life must stop—desist—from its relentless flow so that we can deal with the crisis at hand. But life pays no attention to these crises, so celebrations come and go, seasons come and go, and life marches on, never slowing its pace until you can catch up.

That day, I realized there was an element of this disease that was evil. Jesus promised to give life and give it abundantly (John 10:10 NKJV); He promised that He had not given us a spirit of fear, but of power, love, and a sound mind (2 Timothy 1:7 NKJV). He told us that the enemy comes to steal, kill, and destroy (John 10:10 NKJV). This disease was stealing my husband, destroying his very life and killing our life together. I knew deep within and unequivocally that even if the enemy was involved in this, Jesus had permitted what He could have prevented, and He had good reason for allowing this. Nevertheless, the third entity that had entered into our home from time to time must be resisted.

I ran often to James 4:7–8: "Submit therefore to God. Resist the devil and he will flee from you. Draw near to God and He will draw near to you" (NASB). I submitted to God. What did I submit? I submitted John, I submitted myself, and most difficult of all, I submitted to the trial as Jesus submitted Himself to the trial. He was pliable in His Father's hands, trusting that His Father loved Him and was in complete control, even when it seemed that all the world was out of control. If I was serious about my heart's desire to have the power of His resurrection, I, also, must submit to the fellowship of His sufferings (Philippians 3:10). Strange that these two concepts—fellowship and suffering—would be linked. Fellowship in the Greek is *koinonia*: partnership. I was seeing that partnership with Jesus would include suffering in this world, just as He experienced.

Next, as the Scripture says, I must resist the devil. Given our current culture of tolerance, I wondered if it seemed strange to some to hear talk of the devil. Does anyone still believe there is a person of evil who is out to destroy us, who crouches as a lion waiting for his prey? The Bible says it is so. To ascribe evil to a disease, the stealing away of the invisible parts of the mind, memory, behavior, personality, seems almost medieval to many. Yet, this is how it came to me. There were now three of us living here: myself, John, and this heinous disease. When I wanted to talk to John, it pushed its way in, right in the middle of the conversation. When I needed reassurance and affection, it closed the door in my face and sent my affectionate husband into another room of his mind, ignoring my cries.

And so, the next spiritual principle of James 4 was resisting of this enemy. There was no way around it: Jesus called us to resist steadfastly, not passively. My resisting lay in refusing to listen to the lies I heard spoken in the middle of the night, awaking from a dead sleep. The sense of foreboding and dread sent me immediately to my little prayer closet, where I learned deep and profound mysteries from the Lord. I began slowly to accept the truth of passages such as:

> That He would grant you, according to the riches of His glory, to be strengthened with power through His Spirit in the inner man; so that Christ may dwell in your hearts through faith; [and] that you, being rooted and grounded in love, may be able to comprehend with all the saints what is the breadth and length and height and depth, and to know the love of Christ which surpasses knowledge, that you may be filled up to all the fulness of God. Now to Him who is able to do exceeding abundantly beyond all that we ask or think, according to the power that works within us, to Him [be] the glory in the church and in Christ Jesus to all generations forever and ever. Amen. (Ephesians 3:16–21 NASB)

I have always loved and believed that passage in Scripture, but now it was being worked into my character, as Oswald Chambers says, "worked out in actualities." The questions that came to me in these night watches were: Is this passage true? Is it really true that God grants me, according to the riches of His glory, to be strengthened with power through His Spirit in my inner self? Is it possible that I, a lone housewife from Podunk, Arizona, can comprehend with the saints—with Elijah, Moses, Abraham, and Paul—the multidimensionality of God who is outside of time, space, and matter? Is it possible in the midst of crushing trials to step outside of my framework of time, space, and matter and enter into a supernatural peace and rest in my inner self?

These were weighty issues, but they were real, and they were being worked out in my actuality at that moment, to understand without fear that there is another dimension where an entity called the devil and his host of evil powers exists, scheming and plotting. God of the universe entrusted me to stand up and say to that enemy, "No, that is a lie and I resist it. God is truth, and Jesus has covered that in His blood." In the quiet of those midnight watches, I submitted and I resisted the devil. I drew near to God, and He drew near to me.

CHAPTER TEN

Do Not Be Anxious for Your Life

(Journal Entry 12/16/05)

Ah, this abiding life! The lessons are not in the big events but in the smallest things.

I got it into my head that I needed to find a job, so I could invest money in ways that would help support us in the event John had to leave work. There was nothing wrong with this thought in the natural, but when I sought God's will, I simply heard, "Invest in Me, Kathy." And then, once again, the gentle reminder,

> "For this reason I say to you, do not be anxious for your life, [as to] what you shall eat, or what you shall drink; nor for your body, [as to] what you shall put on. Is not life more than food, and the body than clothing? Look at the birds of the air, that they do not sow, neither do they reap, nor gather into barns, and [yet] your heavenly Father feeds them. Are you not worth much more than they?" (Matthew 6:25 NASB)

God didn't seem to be exasperated in having to remind me of this truth; He just lovingly placed it before my eyes whenever my focus was getting off track.

For the entire week before Christmas, John seemed almost his old self. Not the laughing, teasing self, but confident, in control, and cognizant. I enjoyed it so much, yet I was wary. I had begun to learn not to trust completely this shifting back and forth. I tried not to let my emotions switch gears every time the scene changed at home, but I couldn't help it this time. I wanted my husband back. I didn't care if it was only for a few days; I just wanted him back.

We decided to take a little trip down to Skull Valley and to our little country store with the worn wooden floors and the pickled eggs. The psalmist wrote, "Oh that I had wings like a dove! For then I would fly away and be at rest" (Psalm 55:6 NASB). As soon as the city disappeared behind us and the road began to weave around toward those wonderful cottonwoods, it felt like that, like I was flying away and my soul could rest. Memories flooded my mind like a movie playing before my eyes. I remembered the times we pulled off the road near Kirkland and drove down into the huge rock formations to take pictures. (I later made one of those pictures into a poster with the verse on it about Jesus being our Rock.)

I remembered another drive, and my mind searched for that little dirt cow path, where we came upon an oasis of a stream of water hidden beneath tall cottonwoods and had a spontaneous picnic on the spot. I remembered stopping at the steakhouse in Kirkland and discovering the most wonderful steaks ever. So, on this day, we decided to drive on down to Wickenberg, where memories—sweet, bitter, and fresh—of our trips washed over me. I never wanted to go home. I wanted to steal John away from this disease, which hadn't seemed to follow us here, and start all over again, as if this thing hadn't invaded our lives. But, as Oswald Chambers says, we can't remain on the mountaintop; we must return to the devil-possessed valley. Driving back up the mountain, I decided to put this new memory into my hiding place, into the place where Jesus dwells, and trust Him to keep it safe for me there.

Christmas came and went, not one I care to remember. Adam's sadness over his losses of the past two years dwelt heavy on me. His painful divorce had changed the dynamics of Christmas, making this Christmas without his family very painful. Dane and Tasha were doing well with Dane's business, so Christmas morning at their house was enjoyable. Still, I was glad to have it all behind me.

On December 28, John had his appointment at Barrow's. The new cognitive specialist agreed with the earlier diagnosis but wanted to do further testing on the thyroid and the colloid cyst and run an EEG.

A day before this test, John and I were driving to the mall, when he fixated on a hawk flying overhead. Driving fifty miles per hour toward cars stopped at the stoplight, he lost focus on all else but the hawk and did not notice he was bearing down on the car stopped in front of us. I screamed at him to stop and he did, just at the right moment. Showing absolutely no sign of fear or alarm that we had nearly crashed, he continued on as though nothing had happened, a typical MCI behavior. I related this to the doctor. Alarmed that John was driving, he strongly urged him to stop. Again, John seemed not to hear this warning and insisted on continuing. I had to take that to the abiding place in Jesus and trust Him to keep us safe. These little acts of faith, so small yet so huge, were all a part of the building blocks of this faith walk. I would need all of them for the months ahead.

CHAPTER ELEVEN

God Is Faithful

(Journal Entry 1/2/06)

2006 has arrived. New Year's went without a hitch, but what a year 2005 has been. What does this year hold in store? Never mind—had I known ahead of time what 2005 held in store I would have found a dark closet somewhere and hid out alone. Thank You, Jesus, that You don't allow us to see the future.

I spent a few days at Adam's after Christmas and found a reprieve. Mom went with me, and she, too, felt relaxed and at peace. My prayers there took on added dimension, and my mind cleared, making me aware of how difficult all of this had been and how cloudy my own mind became at times when dealing with John's disease. Back home, however, the oppression grew worse than ever. Discouragement set in, along with doubts and dark thoughts. All those promises I had so believed God had given specially to me—my prayers for my husband to be filled with the Holy Spirit, to step up as the spiritual head of our home—yet I was now being forced to take over more and more of our daily decisions, as John disappeared into this mist of dementia. *Did I hear you wrong, Lord? When I heard last summer that You were going to do a new thing, did I hear You wrong? What was all this for?*

However, as was now becoming God's custom of presenting me with just the right word at just the right time, David Wilkerson's *Pulpit Series* sermon came in the mail and shattered the darkness with a piercing light. The title of his sermon, "God Is Faithful," related the experiences of those who were enduring the greatest time of testing in their lifetimes: "The hardest, most painful time in our lives." They seemed to be set up as targets of the enemy's wrath, as he infuses their thoughts with fear, discouragement, temptation, and depression. Wilkerson exhorts his readers to take a stand on God's Word when faced with these painful times:

> Thou wilt keep him in perfect peace whose mind is stayed [fixed] on thee; because he trusteth in thee. Trust ye in the Lord forever: for in the Lord Jehovah is everlasting strength. (Isaiah 26:3–4 KJV)

Throughout history, many great servants of God ended up feeling they failed in their calling; they are despondent, because they haven't experienced the promise God made to them. All they can see is failure. And now they're crushed, wounded in spirit. They think, *Lord, has all this been in vain? Did I hear the wrong voice? Have I been deceived? Has my mission ended up in ruins?* Capturing what my own heart was crying, Wilkerson goes on to encourage the saints who find themselves in this precipice of faltering faith, reminding us that it is the devil lying to us, telling us that all we've done is in vain, that we'll never see the fulfillment of expectations. But God has, in His glory, prepared a greater blessing and has better things in store, beyond anything we could think or imagine. We are to rise up from our despair and stand on this word: "Be ye steadfast, immovable, always abounding in the work of the Lord, forasmuch as ye know that you labor is not in vain in the Lord" (1 Corinthians 15:58 KJV).

As I read David's message, Jesus came alongside me and brought comfort and encouragement to my wounded soul. I didn't know what my future held. I didn't know what God was doing or was going to do. "Only You, Jesus, only You, matter."

CHAPTER TWELVE

More World Events: Learning the "Rest" of God

(Journal Entry 1-5-06)

Behold, what I have built I am breaking down, and that which I have planted I am plucking up, and this means the whole land. And do you seek great things for yourself? Seek them not: for behold, I will bring evil upon all flesh, says the Lord; but your life I will give to you as a snatched up prize of war wherever you go. (Jeremiah 45:4-5 AMP)

Last summer, on the Jewish celebration of the fast of the ninth of Av, the anniversary of the destructions of both Jewish temples by enemies, Ariel Sharon, Prime Minister of Israel, drove his fellow Jews out of their homes and into a bleak and unknown future. Nine thousand Jews were expelled from their homes, not by Nazi soldiers, but by their own countrymen, by their fellow Jewish soldiers, all of them sobbing and lamenting over such a tragedy. In the end, Israel's enemies entered these fine homes and businesses of the Gaza and completely destroyed every last vestige of Jewish history. Everything was destroyed, every synagogue burned. The famous greenhouses, left behind by the Israelis to help the Gazan's establish their own infrastructure, were destroyed. Anarchy reigned. Youth carrying machine guns roamed the streets killing and looting, and the media reported not one word of this travesty.

My own heart bled for this, drawing me into intercession for God's chosen land, *Eretz Yisrael: The Land of Israel.* In some mysterious way, these events and my own intersected, for I believe that the trials we face today, the severe discipline of learning to trust Jesus with everything, is for the purpose of facing what is certain to come in our future as the unfolding of God's prophecies takes place. Michael Wells aptly said, "Jesus is coming, and He is raising up the lesser man for the greater day." (*Abiding Life Basic Seminar*. Michael Wells. 1988. DVD.)

It may appear odd that I write of these world events side by side with events in my little world. Thus, I include these world events in my writing and find no contradiction in doing so. I am convinced that these weighty issues of the world are ordered by the hand of God and that we, like Daniel, are involved in the unfolding of these plans through prayer. Daniel had an encounter with the archangel Gabriel, who informed him that his prayers had been heard for the nation Israel three weeks earlier, when he had prayed them. But Gabriel had been involved in a cosmic battle with a principality he called the "Prince of Persia" for three weeks.

This unseen battle hindered him from getting to Daniel with the answer. I believe this peek into the unseen dimension, where these forces battle it out, gives us insight into why our lives are intrinsically interwoven with these very events and why we sometimes experience within our own spirits the shifts taking place in the cosmic realms. Jesus pointed out that we are to understand the book of Daniel: "'Let the reader understand'" (Matthew 24:15 KJV). In His teachings on prayer, He included, "'Thy will be done on earth as it is in heaven'" (Matthew 6:10b KJV), implying that there is a divine will already accomplished in heaven, and we on earth are given a supernatural ability to pray His divine will down to earth. And so, these world events are a part of my own life and my own intercession. I have no problem believing that we are all given the same commission as Daniel and Elijah: to be vessels through which the resurrected Jesus Christ can operate in bringing His will to pass.

And so I absorb His lessons on the subject of biblical "rest." Waiting for new tests to be scheduled, waiting for each new doctor to call and give us further instructions proved to be the straw that inevitably broke the camel's back each time, as I waited for calls that never came. No one seemed to know what was taking place, no one seemed to want to take responsibility, and no one seemed to care whatsoever that our lives were on hold while we waited to hear from them. Added to this frustration was the constant insurance paperwork and the threat that certain tests and bills would not be covered. I spent countless hours calling insurance companies and hospitals to schedule tests, only to learn that they would not be covered at one place but would be at another.

In the meantime, we had to get our financial ducks in a row—durable and medical powers of attorney, living wills, and so on. I did most of it myself with my own legal software. All of these decisions came about as I lay in bed, wide awake in the middle of the night, hashing over what I should do next and when I should do it. I thought I was turning these things over to the Lord, asking for Him to give me the guidance I would need for each step, until one night in the middle of yet another exercise of mental gymnastics, I heard Him distinctly ask, "You have given this to me, haven't you? Now can you *rest* in Me? Can you enter into My rest?" Well, this was altogether different, and I knew it was a new revelation of an old truth.

I began to think a lot about the "rest" of God. I looked it up in many passages in Hebrews (NKJV), and found that it had great significance:

Hebrews 3:11 "So I swore in my wrath, They shall not enter into my rest."

Hebrews 3:18 "And to whom swore he that they should not enter into his rest, but to them that believed not?"

Hebrews 4:1 "Let us therefore fear, lest, a promise being left us of entering into his rest, any of you should seem to come short of it."

Hebrews 4:3 "For we which have believed do enter into rest, as he said, As I have sworn in my wrath, if they shall enter into my rest: although the works were finished from the foundation of the world."

Hebrews 4:4 "For he spoke in a certain place of the seventh day on this wise, And God did rest the seventh day from all his works."

Hebrews 4:5 "And in this place again, If they shall enter into my rest."

Hebrews 4:8 "For if Jesus had given them rest, then would he not afterward have spoken of another day."

Hebrews 4:9 "There remains therefore a rest to the people of God."

Hebrews 4:10 "For he that is entered into his rest, he also has ceased from his own works, as God did from his."

Hebrews 4:11 "Let us labour therefore to enter into that rest, lest any man fall after the same example of unbelief.

What did it mean that I should fear lest I should not enter this rest, that my not entering was unbelief? We who have believed do enter into rest, and it is the rest that God Himself entered into at creation! Jesus gives us rest *now*, not someday, if we choose to enter into it. There remains a rest to the people of God. Rest is *Shabbat*—a Sabbath. Rest is ceasing from our works, however we must "labor" to enter into that rest. Because this seemed so important to God—this entering into His supernatural rest—I must not ignore what He said to me on this subject. Faith believes that He *can* take care of everything; rest trusts that He *will*. This thought percolated within my soul for many months. I wanted this rest. I desperately needed this rest.

All of these things—my need for peace and then the surrendering of that peace to situations, the "rest" of God—were teachings I had always believed but were now being made real in my experience. I never for a minute suspected that I was so filled with unbelief, even while I had taught these things to others for many years. It surprised me to learn how many times I succumbed to unbelief instead of rest. Worry is unbelief. Fear is unbelief. But I had a right to worry, didn't I? My life was coming undone, my husband was fading away, everything I had believed and trusted was being tested to the limit. So, didn't I have a right to times of worry and fear? Apparently not, according to God's economy. Again and again, the questions were raised in my mind: Is it true, or is it not? Do I really believe it, or do I not? I had to choose again and again to believe—to trust—no matter my circumstances, no matter my emotions. I must choose to trust and to rest, even when there is no reason left to do so.

CHAPTER THIRTEEN

You Have Managed My Affairs/I Must Be Weak

(Journal entry 1/9/06)

God has me in a place of waiting right now."You heard my voice [then]: [Oh] hide not Your ear [now] at my prayer for relief. You drew near on the day I called to You; You said, Fear not. O Lord, You have pleaded the causes of my soul [You have managed my affairs and You have protected my person and my rights]; You have rescued and redeemed my life! (Lamentations 3:56–58 AMP)

Finally, we got the EEG and CT scheduled in Phoenix. The EEG was a sleep-deprived test, so John was only allowed five hours of sleep the night before. Of course, *he* got five hours; I had practically none. (By this time I was learning to get by on less and less sleep.)

We arrived at the hospital at 6:30 for the first test and learned that the EEG was on the schedule, but not the CT. After many phone calls between the hospital and the doctor's office with no resolution, a kind nurse from the CT lab came out and told us she would get us in right then if we had the doctor's order for the CT. I had it my file that I always carried with me, and the test was done.

While John was having the EEG, I felt panic rising up and called Adam, who was on his way to work. He prayed an anointed prayer for me, and my peace returned immediately. I realized this process was teaching me to appreciate and rely more and more on God's people. We are all intertwined, silent building blocks in this thing called the body of Christ, not just locally, but internationally. It is a joyous and sacred thing. I had so much to learn. I had been a strong person, but what I mistakenly believed was "overcoming" life was actually self-sufficiency. I had always believed God allowed these trials to make us stronger, but I was not becoming stronger: I was becoming weaker. It felt like God Himself was making me weak, stripping me of all my own strength and ability to endure, and that He was leaving me in that weakened state without offering His strength. What a shock it was to realize that He, indeed, was allowing me to become weak because, as Paul wrote:

> And He said to me, "My grace is sufficient for you, for My strength is made perfect in weakness." Therefore most gladly I will rather boast in my infirmities, that the power of Christ may rest upon me. Therefore I take pleasure in infirmities, in reproaches, in needs, in persecutions, in distresses, for Christ's sake. For when I am weak, then I am strong. (2 Corinthians 12:9 NKJV)

What a strange new concept for me: I must be weak in order for His strength to be perfected. I felt awe at this new knowledge, privileged that He was taking such care to teach me these profound truths. If it was true that His strength was perfected *in my weakness*, so be it. I am content to be weak.

Later, a woman from my Bible study who worked with John called. She said she heard a conversation that John was in trouble at work; his condition was becoming evident and affecting his job. People were talking about him, saying they thought he was "losing it."

I called the principal, who had worked with John almost from the start of John's teaching career in Prescott twenty years ago. When I told him about John's condition, he was greatly relieved that he now knew the reason for John's perplexing behavior. I asked him if he thought this disease was affecting John's ability to perform his job, and he gently said, "Yes, Kathy, it absolutely is."

I learned they had already met with John, giving him a timetable to improve and if he didn't, they would not renew his contract. I also learned that if he was let go, he would not qualify for a medical disability and would have to take early retirement, which would not be a sufficient amount on which to live.

John hadn't told me about this meeting, hadn't told me he had a deadline for improvement. When I shared with him that I had spoken to his principal, he was shaken. John has always kept his cards close to his chest. I had not been privy to any of his personal dealings at work, so this was a dramatic shift in the dynamics of our relationship. I felt I had invaded his privacy, betrayed him. This feeling would return again and again, as each new event felt to me like I was sneaking around behind his back and spying on him. It did not feel right to me; it was not comfortable. John had always been completely in control of everything in our lives. He had kept many things from me, had been very self-protective of his emotions. It was our way, our routine.

I think now about these little routines couples develop over time and how unstable everything begins to feel when these long-held relationship dynamics suddenly shift. The moorings are unloosed, and nothing feels normal any longer. I knew that death does that, changes all the dynamics of the relationships involved. I remembered my sisters and I fighting to maintain the status quo when Dad was dying. This rock of a man, who worked so hard to keep the family ties strong, was leaving us, and who would take up the helm? We had gone to a Christian concert during that time, and they sang a song about the "Anchor" holding. I remembered repeating that to myself as the ground was shifted under my feet: "The Anchor holds."

And now, the other rock of a man in my life was no longer able to maintain the status quo. Once more, the ship was listing, and who was going to take the helm? When Dad was dying, I turned to God, but I also turned to John, who was a rock for me. Now, again, I had to make a choice—not daily, but moment by moment—to trust, to rest, and to believe that my Rock was enough.

CHAPTER FOURTEEN

You Never Know that Jesus Is All You Need until Jesus Is All You Have

(Journal Entry 1-14-06)

Now the race is on. The deadline for John to improve or lose his job was three months away. Suddenly, it seemed imperative that the doctor make a diagnosis, so we could begin the medical disability procedures. But the long waiting times between the tests and the next appointments to go over the tests, and the predictable getting to the appointment and the doctor having never seen the test results because someone forgot to send them, became a long nightmare.

At the next appointment, the doctor confirmed that the CT showed some atrophy of the frontal lobe and was ready to make his diagnosis of frontotemporal dementia/Pick's disease. The doctor wanted two more tests; a PET scan and a sleep study to rule out sleep apnea were scheduled. So, another round of tests and battles with the insurance company over coverage and where to have the tests done once more occupied my days. As I began to research the medical disability process, I learned that once you were approved, the waiting period would be six months between your last paycheck and your first disability check.

This time, however, fear and panic did not precede peace. It was not a struggle to find peace: it was there already. Jesus took me early one morning to some of my favorite Bible stories. I read about Gideon, a weak and cowardly young man to whom God appeared and called him "a mighty man of valor." God was not referring to Gideon as he was; He was referring to Gideon as He saw what He would make of him. He commanded Gideon to gather an army, and Gideon gathered an army of thirty thousand valiant men. But God, in His mysterious way, wanting Gideon—and us—to know that He is not dependent on numbers, reduced that army to three hundred, and put to flight thousands of enemy troops.

Elijah was commanded to go to the brook Cherith, where he would be fed and given water. After a short time, the brook dried up. What was Elijah to think now? Had God forgotten? But that was only a part of the process for Elijah. We see each of God's deliverances as if they were the end of the process instead of one step along His vast plan. God said to Elijah, "Arise, go to Zarephath, which belongs to Sidon, and dwell there. See, I have commanded a widow there to provide for you" (1 Kings 17:9 NKJV). As he arrived, the widow was gathering her last bit of wheat to make a small loaf for herself and her son. She expected to die, for there was a great famine in the land. Elijah asked her to make him a loaf first and then one for herself and her son, which she seemed willing to do. It was her all, her last, and she obeyed the voice of the Lord as Elijah told her:

> For thus says the LORD God of Israel: "The bin of flour shall not be used up, nor shall the jar of oil run dry, until the day the LORD sends rain on the earth." So she went away and did according to the word of Elijah; and she and he and her household ate for many days. The bin of flour was not used up, nor did the jar of oil run dry, according to the word of the LORD which He spoke by Elijah. (1 Kings 17:14–16 NKJV)

We see this miracle repeated again in Elisha's story of the woman and the cruse of oil that did not run out.

James takes up the story of Elijah several hundred years later, reminding us that Elijah was a man just like us, subject to the same weaknesses, and yet he trusted his God and God heard him. In all these stories the message is clear: God can create something out of nothing, and He can create life out of death.

If these stories are mere fairy tales from an ancient mythological book, I may read them and receive a sense of enjoyment from them, but only a fool would expect that these things are possible today in our bustling modern culture. If they are real stories of real people who had real encounters with the God of the universe, however, and if several hundred years later, another anointed writer takes up the story and tells us these men and women actually had these real-life experiences and we can expect that God has not changed, we ought to pay attention.

Hearing these ancient stories as they related to my current situation, I heard the distinct urging of God telling me that I could trust Him with my finances, just as surely as these men and women had heard Him, because He was the same God. He then reminded me of my parents' version of this miraculous jar of oil and loaf of bread story. Dad had a head injury from WWII, which got progressively worse over the years, causing him to black out for long periods of time and then come to in terrible pain, clutching his head and tearing at his flesh. We grew up watching this with fear but with a sense of awe, because he never complained about the constant headaches he experienced. Finally, the blackouts caused him to retire early, and our family faced an entire year with no income while the disability process was worked out. The bread never ran out, nor the cruse of oil. They never lacked for a thing, and to this day, there is no explanation as to how they managed with three teenaged girls to live with no income. Only God could create money and provisions where there were none.

Armed with all of these ancient and modern-day stories of God's care and provision, I looked at our meager resources and understood completely and without doubt that God would take care of His little sparrows. It was not a jumping up and down moment; it was a quiet understanding that He had spoken.

The following morning in my little prayer room I read, "I will awaken right early [I will awake the dawn]! I will give thanks and praise to You, O Lord, among the peoples: I will sing praises to You among the nations. For your mercy and lovingkindness are great, reaching to the heavens, and your truth and faithfulness to the clouds" (Psalm 57:8–11 AMP). The Hebrew reading of Hebrews 7 would refer to the *Cohen Hagadol*, the high priest forever, who set up the tent of meeting, not erected by human hands, and sitting at the right hand of God in heaven, I saw what I can only describe as a heavenly sight—Jesus, my High Priest, seated at the right hand of the Father. Waves of pure joy washed over me as I held my Bible to my heart and cried.

CHAPTER FIFTEEN

The Secret Place of the Most High

(Journal Entry 3/28/06)

Psalm 91:1–2 "He who dwells in the secret place of the Most High shall abide under the shadow of the Almighty." It is so supernatural to really get hold of this abiding life. One of the things Jesus has burned upon my mind is that the enemy cannot rob my peace unless I surrender it to him.

The new tests were scheduled for February 16 at the Mayo Clinic. Before then, God spoke several things to my heart during a time of extreme oppression that had settled over my house. These key ideas have been part and parcel of the abiding life teachings, and as I wrote them in my journal, they seemed to lodge deep within my mind and stay there.

- What am I focusing on, the voice of the butcher of the sheep (Satan) or the voice of the Shepherd (Christ)?
- Judge all the thoughts and emotions before they get out of control.
- The enemy is working to get my mind on anything but Christ (my mind wanted to focus on the problems, on John, on self-pity).
- I know when I have let my thoughts break through all the barriers that Jesus sets up for my protection and head off the cliff. I lose the peace of God. Judge the thoughts before this happens.

- There are some things in life that if we get on the roller coaster of runaway emotions, we won't be able to get off until we get beat up. Runaway emotions always lead to the feeling of being beaten up.
- Learn to tell the difference between true guilt and false guilt. True guilt is for true sin, false guilt is continuing to feel the same emotion of guilt after I have asked for and been given forgiveness.
- Make the decision to stand against the lying emotions that come against me like a tidal wave. Don't listen to the lying emotions; don't feed them. What we feed will grow, what we starve will die.
- The decision to choose is my choice, God will not make the choice for me. (*Abiding Life Basic Seminar.* Michael Wells. 1988, DVD.)

I was grateful that God gave me these instructions, because the process of going through these tests was draining, and the sleep study, as it turned out, was only a consultation before they could set up the actual study a month later, which would be after our next appointment with the neurologist. Time was running out.

I was beginning to have a little understanding of the children of Israel and their wilderness wanderings. I had my "no water" experiences and I had my "water from the rock" experiences and yet, when the next no water situation would arise, I again struggled to trust that God would provide. I was not a tower of strength. I was not a model of faith. I learned deeply of His love, patience, and mercy as I struggled with each new situation. This time, the decision seemed to be whether to postpone the doctor's appointment until after the sleep study or just not do the sleep study. It was not clear that our insurance would even pay for it.

We had decided to not do this test when Guy and Diane called to tell us about a doctor friend who had a sleep study clinic and agreed to do the study for John within the next week. Again, God intervened, and the study was done before the doctor's appointment.

As it turned out, John did have severe sleep apnea and apparently was not maintaining a normal oxygen level during his sleep. The doctor was persuaded that John's dementia was due to this apnea, and he was now to be fitted with a CPAP sleeping machine. Now, however, the doctor did not want to sign off on medical disability, and it was a gamble whether the sleep machine would actually improve John's symptoms enough for him to continue working. Getting approved for medical disability for sleep apnea is rare, so it seemed that this avenue was now closed.

All of us who had been praying experienced such joy that John could now be healed and his mind returned to normal. However, as the months went by, it became clear that his dementia symptoms were not improving at all; in fact, they seemed in many ways to be worse. John's principal encouraged me to persuade John to submit his resignation and then proceed with retirement, so they would not be forced to cancel his contract. John agreed to that before the deadline.

In the meantime, we decided to seek a neurologist in town and have John's medical records transferred back here. This would alleviate the stress of the constant driving back and forth and the stress of a doctor who never seemed to remember who we were from one appointment to the next. We had our first appointment with the new doctor, who scoffed at the notion that sleep apnea could cause such serious dementia symptoms and encouraged us to begin medical disability immediately. He was not only willing but almost insistent that he fill out his part of the paperwork, but John had applied at several new jobs and was confident he would be able to continue working.

As I walked through my house amid the chaos, I announced that the enemy can't have my peace. Psalm 91, always a favorite, became a new revelation, and I proclaimed that my peace is hidden in the secret place of the Most High God and covered by His shadow. Since then, He has brought Psalm 91:1–2 to my heart and shown me that even the simplest things can be hidden in the secret place of the Most High God. What is that secret place? He hasn't told me exactly, just that it is available to me to hide in, to rest in, to find perfect peace. The enemy comes at me either from my past or from my future. These days, it is from my future—the uncertainty of our financial future—but now I had the secret place of the Most High God, and when these thoughts invaded my mind, I carefully placed them into His place. What a wonderful thing this is. He is not asking me to think about my future. He simply asks me to put it in that place; abide in Him, and everything is safe there. He watches over all of my emotions there, He knows my way in this wilderness, and He manages my affairs.

My fifty-seventh birthday was blessed. My sweet children bought me an iPod, so now I could listen to music and sing to God wherever I was. How many nights had I risen in the night watch to sing to Jesus, and now

I could sit in my favorite rocking chair by the window overlooking the hills and valley below as my heart sang in wondrous praise. I also put parts of the New Testament on it so I could have God's Word, so precious to me, near at all times.

My Wednesday night Bible study was scheduled to end soon for summer break, and I was profoundly aware of how much I would miss these dear women God had placed in my life. The cards and notes they brought to me, their prayers and love overwhelmed me all year. I realized anew that I so need the body of Christ. I have always had my sisters and family as my friends, and, of course, John had been my best friend these past twenty years. But now I knew that all of God's people were my family. Our little Abiding Life Sunday school class ended, as Diane and Guy were led to other areas of ministry. I didn't realize until later how this affected me, how I had grown to depend on this little support group. It was one place where John and I could go and learn together. I continued to travel to an unknown country, not knowing where I was going. This became my new normal. God's ways are not my ways. His ways are higher than my ways, and just as the old patriarchs who trusted in Him no matter what, so I must trust.

Our next appointment with the new neurologist arrived, and he seemed more intent than ever that John begin the disability process. He filled out all the paperwork that same day. John had had two job interviews, and we were waiting to hear the outcomes. He was confident he could continue to work, and I knew I must let this play out according to God's will without trying to influence him either way. I had left it with the Lord that if John got the job before the doctor's appointment, it meant he was supposed to go forward and God knew something I didn't know. If the doctor appointment came before any job offers, we would go ahead with the disability process. When we arrived home, all the paperwork ready to be completed, John had two calls on his cell phone, both from the jobs he had applied for, and both seemed to be offers. They came in at the exact time the doctor was filling in the paperwork.

John was elated.

I hit a wall.

I felt like some cruel joke had been played on me. The next few days were filled with tension for me, as his contract would be up in another month and I had no idea what to do next. John was trying to make contact with the two jobs but kept missing the calls; nothing seemed certain there. My mom suggested that we go ahead and file the paperwork, and if the jobs came through, we could cancel it. That seemed good to me. But John had returned to believing that he was fine, that there was nothing wrong with him and he could continue working.

A sudden weariness overtook me, like a heavy wool blanket settling down and suffocating me. He had once more rebuked me that I needed to, "Stop making all of this up," about his memory. I think I had heard this enough that, at this point, I truly believed him. The jobs he was looking at meant a severe pay cut. I was trying not to make this decision for him; I felt strongly that he needed to make this very important decision himself.

I spent the weekend crying off and on. My peace was gone. The following week, John had still not heard back about the jobs, and as he came in to say good-bye early Wednesday morning, he said, "You know, I think I should just go ahead with the disability." As soon as the words came out, I felt something physically leave the room and peace flood in. Later, when he got home, I started to say, "You know, this morning when you said that about the job, I felt—" He finished my sentence, "Peace? So did I. I really believe this is what God wants me to do." He went on to tell me that God had broken him, humbled him in all of this. We hugged, and for the first time in a long time, I felt close to him. It seemed that in the process of this brain disease, God left his spiritual life intact, and there was a deep work going on there: a mysterious work.

CHAPTER SIXTEEN

Abiding and Resting in the Midst of Furious Activity

(Journal Entry 5-30-06)

May, always the busiest month of year for us—birthdays, Mother's Day, and end of school year activity—found us engulfed in myriad functions.

Adam bought a new house and was in the throes of the last-minute rush to get his house ready to sell. Dane happened on a great deal on a parcel of land, and he, too, was occupied with numerous business arrangements. I had left the disability paperwork on the counter for John to fill out. but he hadn't touched it in a week. Then, I realized that he wasn't just procrastinating. He actually could not do it. This was the executive functioning, some mysterious hidden part of his brain that was no longer able to do what had always come so easily to him.

We went to Phoenix to help Adam with his house repairs and celebrate his, John's, and my niece Nat's birthdays at her house. John was unusually childlike, excited, and anxious about his birthday, asking repeatedly whether anyone had gotten him any cards or presents. The old John always huffed and puffed, not wanting any attention on his birthday, so this was new behavior. I noticed that he had become unusually emotional; his eyes teared up at the simplest things, things that would not normally cause anyone to cry, let alone this man who never cried.

After the weekend, I began tackling the disability paperwork. I had to chuckle that all of the hassles of the past year, which caused me to collect all of John's medical records from each doctor, now made it much easier to fill in the reams of paperwork. All of the information was readily at my fingertips, and I thanked God for His going ahead of me and preparing this way. I left only a few sections about his educational background and field of study for John to complete. He then only had to sign his name. This simple task threw him for a loop, and again, I was amazed at how this part of his brain could so completely forget the most basic tasks.

After much struggle and arguing, he filled in the information but, when I went to make copies of the document, I saw that he had only filled in his BS degree information and not his MS or field of study. This seemed to completely confuse him, but finally we finished and got the thing mailed. I understood then how things must have been for him at his job, with the mounds of paperwork that needed to be filled in every day on each student. This must have felt like an overwhelming task. No one knew he left it undone not because he was being lazy but because he really couldn't do it.

CHAPTER SEVENTEEN

The Reality Train

(Journal Entry 6/7/06)

I went to an Alzheimer's support group. I was not prepared for the overwhelming emotion that hit me full on like a train.

The train was reality—not the murky confusing world of half make-believe and half-reality where John and I lived, but full-on reality of what our future held. People in the group were in all stages of caretaking. There was a full range of emotions in that room: guilt, fear, resignation, anger, grief, and sorrow. When it came time to share my own story, my emotions imploded, gushing out in a blubbering flood. Not being one who cries easily, and rarely in front of anyone, it felt safe to do it here. However, once the floodgates were opened, they raged out of control for the next several days, and it scared me. My pain scared me.

Later that week, I spoke to the representative from the disability organization, and she told me we would have no problem getting approved. However, we would not receive a check until December 28. That seemed so far away, but in another one of God's amazing provisions—because we had to wait until the end of the contract year to file for disability—our normal summer balloon check from the school would still be given to us and would now actually cover at least three months of the six-month waiting period. Had we filed when we wanted to in March, we would have stopped receiving any paychecks at that point. Now we would have summer covered, and there might even be enough in savings to cover the rest. My pain turned to laughter again. God had promised to provide, and He had.

With all of my winter activities now at an end, I looked forward to a long summer, taking it easy, enjoying time alone with John. I felt God had led me to a place of rest for a few months, yet God seemed to delight in surprising me with new revelations. That very first week, God brought a distraught woman to me for discipleship and encouragement. It occurred to me that for the past two years, I had not been involved in any of my normal one-on-one discipleship, and I felt suddenly unsure of myself. I was different now—weak, not strong and confident.

I agreed to meet with this distraught mother and prayed a silent prayer before leaving my house that Jesus would speak to her heart through this broken-down vessel that I had become.

It was a good meeting. Jesus did indeed speak to her, and this began what I later realized was an entirely new journey on this amazing path He had prepared for me. As this new, weak vessel, He could now actually be completely free to speak His own words and show His own love, while I watched in amazement.

Later, I stopped off at the Alzheimer's office to pick up some material. Waiting for the director, I spotted a little book on a shelf about a caregiver's journey through his wife's dementia and asked if I could borrow it. Back home, as I began to read the first few chapters, I knew God had led me to this book and, ultimately, to my introduction into the next phase of this journey with John. Every page spoke as if the writer had peered inside my own private experiences, collected my own pain and hidden fears, and exposed them to my conscious mind. My soul resonated with this writer's pain, and at last, I understood in a deeper way than ever before that God was going to go through this with us. He was crying with us; He had already suffered this pain Himself, and knew what it was, how it felt.

Adam's house had become a respite for me. The caretakers at the support group encouraged me to get away for respite whenever I could. John was not yet unable to care for himself, and so from time to time I could leave for a few days. Alone at Adam's with no phones and no disturbance, I could wake when I wanted, spend all day in my pajamas if I chose, and leisurely read, which I did a few days later, staining each and every page of my new book with my tears. There was something about leaving the familiar four walls of my house, where there was always the next thing to do on my never-ending list.

This time alone proved to be a glorious and peaceful few days for me. As the writer poignantly expressed the very pain I had not been able to express, it gave me permission to hurt. Yet, in the very act of mourning, God Himself was measuring out the number of tears I was to cry—no more, no less. With less, I would be in danger of internalizing the tears, and their toxins would poison my soul. If more, these very tears of healing would become a flood that drowned me. So, He allotted me just enough tears to heal. He also seemed to be urging me to begin writing of my journey down this road. A book perhaps.

I learned in the quiet of my days that Jesus desired for me to learn to be still, to stop thinking and analyzing so much, and to begin allowing myself to live in the moment with John, whose senses now seemed to be drawn into small moments. He reveled in beautiful sunsets and became almost fixated on a nearby overlook where he could view the San Francisco Peaks. Each time he gazed out on a favorite scene, he repeated his total amazement at the view, as though he were seeing it for the first time.

Everything to John became "amazing." "Did you know Dustin Hoffman was born in 1949? Amazing." While my mind was racing off to the next thing on my to-do lists, John's mind had stopped being able to do anything but marvel and be amazed wherever he was at the moment. Jesus was asking me to do this hardest of all things—stop and marvel along with John at the things he found to be amazing. It felt almost like an act of worship. Indeed, it was exactly that. I realized this would be a delicate balancing act. I didn't want my busy life to be merely an interruption in this new life of taking care of John. Neither did I want the events of John's life to be merely an interruption in my daily activities. As I spoke to Jesus later in the night watch, I prayed:

> I cannot do this. You must do this through me. I want this old Kathy— the rushed, impatient Kathy—gone. I don't want to have to think about her or tend to her hurt feelings or drag her nonstop, thinking, analyzing mind to infringe on this sacred holy thing You are doing. Jesus, You are love—come and be love through me. You are peace—come and be peace through me. You are faith—come and be faith through me. And You are gentleness, goodness, kindness, compassion, meekness, and self-control—be all those things through me. Thank You. I receive Your life, living through me. I accept and

believe that because I asked, You will freely give. No good thing will You withhold from those who ask. Dementia is not a good thing. Walking by John's side in his new world with Your eyes is a good thing. Let me see John as You see him.

The following morning God led me to Oswald Chambers' devotional "Abide in Me." It read:

> It does not matter what my circumstances are, I can be as sure of abiding in Jesus in them as in a prayer meeting. I have not to change or arrange my circumstances myself. With our Lord the inner abiding was unsullied. He was at home with God wherever His body was placed … Think of the things that take you out of abiding in Christ—Yes Lord, just a minute, I have got this to do; Yes, I will abide when this is finished; when this week is over, it will be alright. I will abide then. Get a move on; begin to abide now. (Chambers, Oswald. *My Utmost for His Highest*. Uhrichsville, OH: Barbour Publishing, 1963, p. 166)

And so, there it was, in black and white. Still, I was not prepared for what the summer would hold—a different summer than the last. This time, it was with much stillness and rest that I waited.

CHAPTER EIGHTEEN

How Much I Have Already Changed

(Journal Entry 6/27/06)

As I continue writing the book God instructed me to write, it becomes starkly clear how much different my inner self is today than it was a year ago. The changes God has worked in me are miraculous. The peace and contentment, the love and compassion for John—truly, He who began a good work in me is perfecting that work.

Since John's retirement, I began to experience what I can only describe as a supernatural peace, peace that passes all understanding according to Philippians 4:7. I became aware that this thing God calls "rest" is something we choose. Though it feels so elusive, it is elusive only because we are so accustomed to doing everything ourselves, so accustomed to our self-sufficiency that it takes a very long time to even recognize how little we actually depend on Jesus Christ. I'm certain I had experienced bits and pieces of this rest over the course of my life with Christ. I'm not sure I had fully understood, however, that He earnestly desired for me to be utterly dependent on Him, or that He cared so deeply for my well-being, to the point of allowing me to become "rest-deprived" so that I would become desperate for His peace and rest in my life moment by moment, not intermittently.

Now that I had tasted this peace and rest, I never wanted to be without it again. I was immediately aware when it was gone, and when I asked Him to show me where I had surrendered my peace, He quickly showed me.

If the summer of 2005 was an emotional wasteland, 2006 was proving to be my summer of peace, rest, and joy. "'Come unto me, all ye that labour and are heavy laden, and I will give you rest'" (Matthew 11:28 KJV), always a favorite, now became embedded into my experience, into my actuality.

In May, we drove to Tucson to spend a few days. As we approached Mayer, John began pointing out distant mountains, which had apparently been one of his favorite scenes. As he pointed, he began to choke up. I asked him what was making him cry, and he simply said, "I don't know, I'm just becoming so humble." In Tucson, as he related some past event that did not seem particularly sad, he started to cry again. And when he saw that the East Coast had been experiencing flooding, he did the same. This was a new change in his emotions that would repeat itself over and over. Once home, however, as if in defiance of the other symptoms of the disease, he started a detailed house project, which he finished with ease, as though nothing was ever wrong with his ability to do these things.

This disease was so complex, I found myself hating it vehemently. Yet, I realized that anger, too, is part of the grieving process. The problem with going through a grieving process in this fragmented sort of way is that one never gets *through* the process to the end. It occurred to me that I seemed to be going through the whole process over and over again—denial, bargaining, anger, and so on—and I was always surprised to find myself beginning at the beginning, denying that this was happening.

Arizona and the whole of the Southwest were in yet another terrible drought. This year was worse than usual, so it was with great joy when the rains finally came: moisture to our dry parched souls. I was reminded of Psalm 63:1: "God, thou art my God; early will I seek thee: my soul thirsteth for thee, my flesh longeth for thee in a dry and thirsty land, where no water is" (KJV). This had been a dry and thirsty land to be sure; devastating fires had been burning all over the Southwest, Sedona in particular.

July Fourth in Prescott is plain, old-fashioned Americana at its best. Families set up canopies, BBQ grills, and ice chests for the day at Pioneer Park; the aroma of grilled hamburgers and hot dogs hangs heavy in the air. An elaborate children's area of pony rides and helium-filled bouncer toys covers the adjacent ballpark, and makeshift ballgames spring up in the grassy areas. After sundown, the fireworks begin. No matter how many times I see fireworks, they never fail to bring out childlike glee in me.

Again, I couldn't help comparing this summer to the last one, when my heart was so heavy and sad even the fireworks failed to lift my spirits.

On this day, there was a midafternoon downpour, which nearly set our canopy aloft, as it actually did to others around the park. What a sight! "Ezy-ups" were sailing across the field like kites, families running after them oblivious to the lightning flashing all around, food now wet and drippy. But it was over as quickly as it started, and the day was warm and leisurely. The sounds and smells awakened old childhood memories of long, hot, endless summers when I didn't have a care in the world.

CHAPTER NINETEEN

The Spirit Does Not Get Dementia

(Journal Entry 7/10/06)

My days are very full lately but my early mornings with Jesus are so unbelievably precious. He brings such peace and calm to me. However, I have such difficulty on weekends for some reason, which I haven't been able to define.

T hat weekend, I became impatient with John, because he always seemed so anxious to be going somewhere and impatient for me to get ready. Later, I apologized to him and hugged him. He asked me to be patient with him, explaining that he wasn't always aware what he was doing or saying and that he couldn't focus his thoughts and memory. He was finally open and honest about what he was going through, trying to explain what he was hearing from the Lord and tearfully sharing his heart with me. Then, he sat next to me on the sofa and held me. It was so tender and precious; my heart was aching. *O Lord, I want my husband back. This new man seems to be a man You are building in spite of the dementia.* I had forgotten how secure I had always felt with John's arms around me. Because he was so big, I had always felt completely safe when he was near. This would be another memory to hold and treasure in my heart forever.

During this time, God reminded me of one of my prayers a few years before. I had been trying to prune my rosemary bushes and became discouraged as the mass of twisted, woody, dead branches stubbornly refused to budge. As I stood staring at the bush, I could see tiny green shoots trying to peek out from underneath and realized that there was life in that plant. But the dead wood kept the sun from getting to the new growth. I recall vividly telling God that this was like my own life, dead wood, tangled relationships, and stubborn pride all crowding out the new growth trying to peek through. I told Him that this dead wood needed to be uprooted and asked that He begin this process of pruning in our family. He heard that prayer and began almost instantly to cut away the dead wood. Four years later, He was still at it. I was beginning to see those tiny green shoots growing higher, while the dead wood grew smaller.

If there was one important thing I learned in this process, it was that God does indeed do the work when we get out of His way, but His time is not our time. There is what I call the "patience of the saints," which is worked into the process. It is most noticeable when we have prayed earnestly, and our prayers have seemingly hit a brass ceiling. This patience—or I should say, this lack of patience—in us is exposed during the waiting.

My Bible study group normally had a few potluck get-togethers during the summer. I held a special dinner, where a woman from our local Messianic Jewish community taught us Davidic dance. What fun we all had—a bunch of middle-aged (and not so middle-aged) Baptists dancing to Messianic songs!

Soon after that evening, my summer heated up rapidly. There was a prophecy conference in town with my favorite speakers, modern-day versions of Elijah, Zechariah, and Joel, all speaking at the very time Israel was now at war with Hezbollah in Lebanon. In the midst of this, I got calls to meet and pray with several people who were struggling. It seemed that a year after God had asked me to lay it all down, He was bringing service back into my life. I wasn't at all sure I was ready. He was ready, however, and I began to understand that this new abiding life didn't mean sitting passively; it meant being so at rest with Jesus that when the call comes, He moves out and I follow along. When I stay out of the way, He does all the talking and even the praying, and I sit in awe at what I see Him doing in the lives He brings into my path. I also later realized that these times were sent from God to refresh my soul. I learned that my purest joy comes when ministering to other hurting women.

In the meantime, John was growing more calm and tenderhearted. I saw a deepening of his spiritual life taking shape. God seemed to be bypassing John's soul and was ministering directly to his spirit. As I talked this over with Jesus in the quiet of the night watch, He reminded me that the spirit does not get dementia.

John's cousin Julie and Aunt Doris came for a visit. I so enjoyed their company and Christian fellowship, and it lifted John to have them here. The three of them traveled to the Grand Canyon on an overnight trip, and while there, John called to tell me he had bought me something. When he got home, he took me alone to another room, watching excitedly, like a little boy, as I opened the card. It was a sympathy card. It read, "With deepest sympathy … for your loss." After "loss," he had written, "of my mind and memory." I broke down. It was simply more than I could bear, such exquisite pain and love side by side, speaking in a few words of the great depth of pain in his heart of these losses in our lives. He had also picked out a tiny pair of malachite earrings, and it pleased him so to have me wear them.

Julie had experience in cognitive behavior issues, and on the last night of their visit, she took me aside after the others had gone to bed. With tears in her eyes, she told me she thought I was an amazing woman but that I had a very hard road ahead. From a professional standpoint, she felt in some areas John behaved at the level of a ten-year-old, and, of course, I could see that myself. She gave me great practical counsel on things I should begin doing now in preparation for what was to come down the road, including gathering some good friends who could step in for me from time to time to give me a break, because I would need that. She also gave me some ideas on keeping John active and setting up visual helps around the house for him to see our day-to-day activities.

This was hard to hear. It broke my heart, but I knew it was true. I was crying as she told me these things. I was like a frog in the water. The changes were moving along steadily, but I adapted. Whatever changes took place would quickly become my new normal. In fact, I soon forgot what the old normal was.

Having Julie here really brought home the drastic changes in John, because she had known him all his life. She said that the changes even from last summer, when he was in Maryland, were dramatic. I appreciated so much all her counsel on things I hadn't even considered. I was suddenly aware that their visit was from God, just for that purpose.

Soon after they left, our pastor resigned, which meant that my good friend Gwyn would be leaving. I had really grown close to her since we had been teaching together, and I had a sinking feeling of loss when I read the letter from the church. With so many changes happening in my personal life, I longed for stable friendships and relationships, and when those changed, I found that I didn't adjust very quickly. In the past, I had John for my stability in human relationships, along with my sisters and family, and that was all I needed. This past year, I had become more dependent on relationships in the body of Christ, so when that ground began to shift even to the tiniest degree, it felt shaky.

CHAPTER TWENTY

Meribah!

(Journal Entry 7-31-06)

This was the water of Meribah, because the children of Israel contended with the LORD, and He was hallowed among them (Numbers 20:13 NKJV).

On Sunday, we got in my car to leave for church, and it wouldn't go into reverse. Something was wrong with the transmission. I needed the car to go to Phoenix the next day, and suddenly, I crashed emotionally. In spite of the peace and joy I had experienced the past few months, even through a recent brake problem that cost us $160.00, that morning I crashed. It was just the combination of being too busy, not having any time to myself (so important to a "thinker"), learning that Gwyn was leaving, and now transmission problems and not enough money to deal with that. At that moment, I lost my peace. Doubts and fear and a great, great sadness overcame me. We used John's car to get to church. I sat through church, ready to implode.

In the past, John would have opened the car hood, checked the fluids, and at least tried to find the problem. Now he just ignored it, as he had with the brake problem. So, I spent the rest of the day just trying to collect my thoughts and decide what to do. I finally called Adam, and he asked me if I had checked the fluids. He urged me to go out, pop the hood, and check the transmission fluid. While talking to him on the phone, I did that. John discovered it and became very agitated and started pushing me aside while he tried in vain to find the dipstick. It was painful to watch how much he had forgotten about these things. I told Adam that I had to leave it alone, because John was getting too upset.

I came back in the house. By then, I was unable to keep from breaking down. It was a beautiful rainy day, and later there was a huge rainbow, which John wanted us to stand and watch together. I complied but was not feeling much joy. Finally, God showed me that I needed to just let it all go, not worry about getting to Phoenix, and to go to that place of rest He had taught me about so thoroughly this past year. I had fallen back to a place of worrying about the money: how—if we barely could make ends meet for the next four and a half months—could I possibly get the car fixed, why did the car have to break down twice since we started on this interim of no income, and the whole nine yards of worry, doubt, unbelief.

I kept hearing God remind me of the children of Israel who—after all the goodness God had shown them—when faced with a no water situation, they murmured, "Can God prepare a table in the wilderness?" (Psalm 78:19 NASB). I was doing the same thing but couldn't seem to get out from under the great sadness that had enveloped me at that point. I think sometimes I needed to allow myself to be sad, because I needed to cry. He provided opportunities for me to cry, but not in unbelief!

We had the car towed Monday morning, and while John was gone, Dane called, wanting to borrow a tool. He could tell I was down, and when I told him about the car, he said he'd be right over. When he arrived, I was really into a crying jag and told him how sad it was to see John go down, to see him unable to figure out where the dipstick was. I showed him the card John gave me and how much it hurt to hear him apologize to me for his memory loss.

While I was crying, Dane said, "Mom, Tasha and I have made a lot of money over the past several months, and since we haven't found a church home yet, we haven't done anything with our tithe. It has been sitting in this envelope, and we have prayed about where to give it. This morning God told us to give it to you." He handed me an envelope with over $1,000 cash in it! Well, as you can imagine, I really lost it then. Can God provide a table in the wilderness? Indeed He can! Dane went on to tell me that he would always be here for me, to fix our cars and help with anything else I needed. I was not to hesitate to call him.

When John got home, I told him what had happened, and he just held onto me, crying. He said that God spoke to him the day before in the rainbow and, like a little child, he remembered that the rainbow was meant by God to show that the floods would not overcome us anymore.

He had read the story of the flood in Genesis that morning, as well as two different devotionals from Tozer's devotional on the Holy Spirit, which he said God had given him and had shown him the fruit of the Holy Spirit in Galatians 5:22. He said he had prayed to God the Father, God the Son, and God the Holy Spirit to take over our situation. It is difficult to express what an emotional time this was for both of us. It was like God was telling us that He would not allow this flood to overtake us, and we would get through it together, with Him.

After that, I really was at rest, although contrite that I had doubted. I kept telling myself that I wasn't doubting God but that I was just discouraged. Then God gently showed me through Chambers devotional:

> "Suppose God has brought you up to a crisis and you nearly go through but not quite, He will engineer the crisis again," and, "Never quench the Spirit, and do not despise Him when He says to you—'Don't be blind on this point any more; you are not where you thought you were. Up to the present, I have not been able to reveal it to you, but I reveal it now.' When the Lord chastens you like that, let Him have His way. Let Him relate you rightly to God.

> "Nor faint when thou art rebuked of Him." We get into sulks with God and say—"Oh well, I can't help it; I did pray and things did not turn out right, and I am going to give it all up." Think what would happen if we talked like this in any other domain of life!

> Am I prepared to let God grip me by His power and do a work in me that is worthy of Himself? Sanctification is not my idea of what I want God to do for me; sanctification is God's idea of what He wants to do for me, and He has to get me into the attitude of mind and spirit where at any cost I will let Him sanctify me wholly. (Chamber, Oswald. *My Utmost for His Highest*. Uhrichsville, OH: Barbour Publishing, 1963, p. 227)

I went to Phoenix later that afternoon in John's car. He still had the van, so he wasn't without transportation. The car ended up costing less than $200, but the lesson was priceless! The message God gave me about Elijah and the widow became a reality in my life. We had started the summer with some money in savings and our summer balloon pay, but on paper, it looked pretty dismal. Certainly, there would not be enough to last until the end of December, when we were told we would get our first disability check. I deposited enough in the checking account from the summer paycheck to cover bills through August and kept the rest in cash in an envelope in my desk drawer to cover gasoline and groceries. Amazingly, we never did without. I paid a few doctor bills in full and used part of it to fix the brakes on the car, and I hadn't even counted to see what was left. When I counted it later (not including Dane's money), there was more left over in that envelope than I had ever had at the end of summer. It was the "cruse of oil" happening right before my eyes. This was my Meribah, no water situation, and doubts and discouragement when the transmission broke had surfaced yet again. After God had done such amazing things for us, after He made sure that the entire $4,000 Mayo Clinic bill was paid in full by the insurance, even after having company for a week and spending more than we would have spent otherwise, when that crisis with the car hit, I did the old children in the wilderness routine. But that, too, was part of the process God allowed.

We left for Phoenix the following day to help Adam pack for his move. The time in Phoenix was more than blessed. Helping Adam pack went smoothly, and the move went without a hitch. John enjoyed helping, and whereas the old John would have been complaining and barking orders and huffing and puffing through the whole thing, the new John rarely complained about anything. He had an extraordinary amount of patience now. Amazing.

At the end of August, John and I decided to take a short trip to Flagstaff. Again, there was so much tension involved in preparing for this trip, so unlike our old days when we both went about our business excitedly and then that wonderful feeling of finally pulling out of the driveway ready for a new adventure. Things that John always did he no longer remembered, and my doing them seemed to annoy him. This time, he hadn't turned on the refrigerator in the RV so it would be cool when we put the food in. When I asked him if he had done it, he said no, and when I asked him if he would do it, as he was walking out the door with the food in his hands, he said no.

There was a momentary flare-up, and he rushed across the kitchen toward me, shouting for me to shut up, with the same angry look of the previous summer. As he got right upon me, he raised his hand as if to hit me but caught himself before he actually did.

He then became weepy and apologetic and begged me to finish getting ready to go. But I could only cry. Everything drained right out of me. The knowledge that this anger lies just beneath the surface of his emotions is the most frightening thought I could imagine. To know that there is no longer that automatic stopping point, or that I can't gauge what might trigger it, is terrifying. To have a six-foot, two hundred sixty-pound man looming over me, knowing that his brain no longer functions the way it should, and not knowing where it will end up, and worse, that there was nowhere I could go, no way I could call for help at that moment, brought the stark reality that this faith walk meant I now had to depend on Jesus to protect me physically from my once loving husband. My John would never have done this. Never.

His pleading finally wore me down, and I reluctantly went on the trip. Driving into Flagstaff later, he pulled into oncoming traffic, going the wrong way. I knew then that I could no longer drive with him. It didn't faze him. He passed it off as simply a mistake; everyone makes mistakes. This was a major decision for us. It now meant I would drive if we went anywhere together, and he hated that. It was to be one of the most difficult decisions I had to make, yet not as difficult as the one I would have to make sooner or later: to have him stop driving altogether. I left that one with the Lord; I could not force John to stop driving by myself. It would have to be divine intervention.

CHAPTER TWENTY-ONE

I Have Nothing to Bring to This Table, Lord

(Journal Entry 9/6/06)

*Bible study resumed on September 6 and my heart swelled
with pure joy at seeing my women again. My days are very
full. The cruse of oil did not run dry and there was money left
over in the grocery budget after three months of summer.*

Ministry became a joy—the only place where there was joy in my life.
Whereas, last year I couldn't imagine discipling and teaching on
top of this ordeal with John, now God Himself went ahead of me, and I
simply followed. It didn't matter if I was in an emotional heap; when the
call came, He just asked me to show up and watch. He was faithful to pour
out through me, through my pain, and I came home grinning ear to ear.

If I could even begin to stretch the tangled emotions I felt into a
straight line, they possibly could wrap around the world. There is the joy
of meeting with the women God brought into my life, witnessing the Holy
Spirit speaking to their hearts, to their pain, through my own voice—yet
not I, but Him. And as I watched their eyes light up and their hearts open
to the depths of Jesus Christ, I was filled with amazement and awe, for I
knew it was only He doing this, and that He allowed my constant pain
and brokenness to remain so His strength could be perfected. Therefore,
I could boast in my weakness.

Then there was the polar opposite emotions of overwhelming sadness
and grief and unanswered prayers, not knowing how all of this would
end. And there was the secret part, the part I never discussed with anyone
and can barely mention now, but it must be so with all caretakers in this

situation. I wanted my husband back, but in his state of mind, I wanted God to take him home, so I wouldn't have to watch this thing unfold to its natural conclusion. This could never be reconciled. I could not stuff these emotions, as they would surely surface later once I was alone. And, I knew that if Jesus did not take them now, they would destroy me.

During this time, John brought in a journal he had kept in 2002, the year my niece died. While I had been in Phoenix that week, waiting long, sleepless hours in the hospital waiting room and grieving over her death, he never came to be with me. I felt so lonely for him at that time and couldn't understand why he hadn't come. Being an only child and having no children of his own, sharing did not come easily to him. If he liked a book and I wanted to read it, I had to buy my own. He kept his personal life and things to himself. He kept his faith to himself as well. Now he handed me this journal, and I cried as I read the scriptures he had been praying for Jennifer. All he had shared with me during that terrible time was impatience that our summer vacation was being interrupted. But, his journal told something completely different. It felt like a microcosm of our lives together, the stark difference between our outer lives and John's inner life that I never got to see.

Looking back, I realized again the contradictions of our lives. It was like we had two lives: the outward, fun-loving life and the dark side I never knew. Now that his brain was closing me off even more, it only added to the mystery of John. Though he had seemingly lost the ability to function normally, he still read his Bible every morning, along with his Tozer devotionals, and seemed to have comprehension of it all.

I knew I must leave these things with Jesus, and He could see into John's brain and knew exactly what was going on there. While I know that all of this is for my pruning and training, I sometimes forgot that it was for John's pruning and training also. In all of this, Jesus reminded me that He was near and listening. I was still to sing and pray, but I was also to stand guard. Warfare when necessary, abide steadfastly.

CHAPTER TWENTY-TWO

Government Programs/God's Provisions

(Journal Entry 11/2/06)

Back to the hassles with the government programs. We qualified for temporary state-assisted health care but it is not as simple as I thought. Everyone tells me something different and I do not know how to maneuver my way around the system.

John had what appeared to be a hernia in his stomach. We had applied for assistance, since our insurance was canceled during our waiting period for disability, and the monumental red tape and endless phone calls yielded only partial answers and much frustration. When our family doctor said he wouldn't be covered, I finally just said, "Never mind. John doesn't need to see a doctor," and hung up. It wasn't anger; it was just a weary sadness that came down every time we faced another obstacle in this process.

John was also hammering me with questions I couldn't answer. These daily annoyances—dealing with the medical and government system and John's inability to understand any of it—though they seem small in retrospect, always took me down. The stress of dealing with the disease was manageable as long as other things went smoothly, but when they didn't, I felt defeated. It helped when a friend in Tucson, whose husband had the same disease, called, and we shared the details of our crazy up and down lives. Note to self: caretakers desperately need to talk to others who are facing these insurmountable hurdles.

The morning following my telephone call to our family doctor, they called back to apologize, explaining they had made a mistake and would be covered after all. They got him in that afternoon and then referred him to another doctor, who would check the hernia. Again, we waited. There was something mysterious about this exercise in waiting on the Lord that was more important than I could have known with my finite mind. But God was educating me, and I knew it was also important to Him.

Christmas was coming. I was very much at peace about not being able to buy the usual mountain of gifts. I found that I was looking forward to enjoying the other parts of the season, such as decorating and getting together with friends.

At the next Bible study the ladies presented me with an envelope stuffed with $500.00 in cash. Oh Lord, how I love these ladies. Earlier, an anonymous giver left a gift card for a grocery store in our church mailbox. God bless these friends.

Later, I attended the Alzheimer's support group to hear a local doctor who specialized in dementia and their caregivers. He was not a neurologist, but his approach was practical and caring, not merely clinical. It was so refreshing to hear all he had to say, and I had the suspicion that he was a Christian, who saw his practice as much as a ministry as a medical practice. He described what I had already experienced—that most neurologists rely too heavily on tests and not enough on listening to the patient and the caretaker.

The usual memory test given by the neurologists is the Mini-Mental State Examination (MMSE), which evaluates the stages of dementia. John always performed 29/30 with 30 being the highest score. If that was the test used, John was normal. In fact, as I sat and mentally performed the test with him, I scored much lower. I could not for the life of me start at one hundred, subtract seven, and continue to do the subtraction in my head. For someone like John, however, who had a sharp mind for mathematics and had, as a special education teacher, given many of these same kinds of tests to students, there were many years of practice behind him. With the mental deterioration I was witnessing at home, and then to watch him perform normally on these tests, I wondered what it would look like when he no longer performed well on them? I could only imagine. I had to come back again and again to one thing: only God knew what was going on in John's brain.

I did notice something new that was indicative of more decline: John had begun to lose words. In describing the trees blowing in the wind, he said they were "flapping." Dane called one day that he was coming over, and when I hung up the phone and told John that Dane was dropping over, as he had some time to kill before his next job, that set off a long and frustrating (for both of us) dialogue about what it was Dane was going to "kill." I tried to explain what I meant simply, but he continued to ask what Dane was going to kill. Thankfully, Dane got there and the conversation changed.

A few days before Thanksgiving, I remembered a humorous conversation that he and a cousin used to have. I tried to remind him of the story, and the more I tried to tell him, the more I laughed. The story had been repeated many times over the years, but now as I sat across the room from him, I looked at him, and he was staring at me, confused and uncomprehending what I was saying. He even seemed surprised at my laughter. I looked away quickly, and my laughter turned instantly into tears. Pure laughter turned into pained grief in an instant.

It hit me full on how long it had been since John and I had laughed together. There are people who laugh and tell jokes and you oblige them by laughing, whether they are truly funny or not. John and his cousin Paul were the two funniest people I have ever been with. Years after one of their hilarious stories, just the memory of their dialogues would still cause me to laugh out loud.

John's exuberance and presence were always bigger than life. *He* was bigger than life; he filled every moment of life with enthusiasm, whether it was a new and exotic recipe, music, or a new repertoire of his never-ending ability to make up off-the-wall words to an old song. Every sign on a billboard would be turned around to mean something new. Sometimes I would be sitting, quietly reading with music playing in the background, and out of nowhere, here would come John, dancing like a ballerina on tiptoe, all six feet, two hundred sixty pounds of him, and I would collapse in laughter.

My emotions over this are now mingled with the dichotomy of the opposite of the laughter. There was also the John who could never show any affection for my sons and grandchildren; the John who kept his own secret, private self completely hidden from me; the John who was not able to show empathy for others, who made fun of the weak; who couldn't even share a book with me. There was the John who couldn't share his faith with others and guarded it like a secret meant only for him and who disdained my more outward sharing of my faith. There was the John who had this wonderful, funny life with me and also seemed to have another life with lots of secrets. There was a John I never knew. Now I never would.

CHAPTER TWENTY-THREE

The Power of His Resurrection/The Fellowship of His Sufferings

(Journal Entry 11/25/06)

What is my fear rooted in? Fear that I can't face John's death;
yet I can't face his life either. Fear that in this interim I will
lose my mind.

The Saturday after a wonderful Thanksgiving at Adam's, I rushed into my prayer corner, desperate for a word from the Lord. I had been listening to Beth Moore CDs for a few months, and she spoke about a "now" word. On this particular morning, my "now" word was "rest today." I heard Him instruct me to be completely silent this day—no TV, no talking, no phone calls—also, to eat light, nonrich foods. I know myself. I know how my good intentions begin well and end badly, so I entrusted this completely to Jesus, and what a day it turned out to be. I asked John to let me be alone, and he did. My mind needed to rest, not think. My soul needed to rest; my body needed to rest.

It was a true Shabbat, ordered by Jesus and carried out by Him. At the end of the day, I was fully restored. This subject of the divine and ordered "rest" of God began to form a kernel of understanding that would germinate and grow over the months.

At my small group a few days later, these seven wonderful couples presented me with an envelope containing $1,400, which would more than carry us through the month of December. I was bowed down with awe and humility as I watched my Father fulfill His promise to this little sparrow so many months ago. In spite of my own failures and poor stewardship, He was merciful and compassionate.

My sister, nieces, and I attended Beth Moore's conference at the beginning of December, each carrying our own package of burdens. The conference ministered refreshment to us, right where we each needed it. The message was timely.

Everything God was allowing in our lives right now was for the purpose of His divine release to increase. The first Adam was told to go forth and multiply; the increase was material and physical. The second Adam sent us forth to increase spiritually, to come to full spiritual maturity. God has invested His purpose in my life; He has invested His plan for my life, His will for my life, and His call for my life. The word I heard directly from God: "There is a *result* I am after in this difficult time." And again, "God has invested humblings in my life—humility is the biggest investment of God in my life—God never ushers us into a new season of increase without first investing in a season of humility. If we take our losses and bury them, they produce no increase; our losses are for our increase."

The Acker festival this year was difficult. Only John and I could go, and while in years gone by, we would have provided our own entertainment, this time he was irritable, impatient to get to hear only one group. He finally erupted with, "Do we have to go into every store?" So, we headed off to hear the one group he had fixated on all evening, and I fought back the tears of the wonderful memories we had had in years before at this festive time. I silently asked, *Lord, what do I do with all these memories? Where can I go to escape them?* Prescott is one long memory — restaurants, driving around town to see new houses, discovering new roads we hadn't been down, driving up to the Pointe (where we were sure we once saw a UFO), warm summer evenings going to TCBY, and sitting outside to watch the summer activities. Or, bundling up at the first snowfall for our traditional drive around town after sunset, and getting out and walking just to hear the crunch of snow under our boots. This in-between place between life and death tormented me; my old memories seemed to collide head on with what John was now. I missed the laughter, the warm hugs, and the mad drives.

This loss created a craving to do something new to make new memories, and I needed my family around me. So, the next day we all decided to go see the movie *Nativity Story* and then drive through the Christmas light show and back to the house for coffee and hot chocolate. That more than made up for the disappointing Acker night. It felt good to have my house filled with children and laughter.

I had recently been pondering Philippians 3:10 (NKJV), Matthew 21:21(KJV), and Galatians 2:20 (KJV), as follows:

> that I may know Him and the power of His resurrection, and the fellowship of His sufferings, being conformed to His death …

> Verily I say unto you, If ye have faith, and doubt not, ye shall not only do this which is done to the fig tree, but also if ye shall say unto this mountain, Be thou removed, and be thou cast into the sea; it shall be done.

> I am crucified with Christ: nevertheless I live; yet not I, but Christ liveth in me: and the life which I now live in the flesh I live by the faith of the Son of God, who loved me, and gave himself for me.

I had been asking God about this thing He called the power of His resurrection. What was this power? I knew it was related to His sufferings, and if one desires that power, one must also submit to the fellowship of His sufferings.

I began to think about the power of the resurrection, and God gave me a new revelation of this old text. Jesus Christ who dwells in me, who abides in me, is the resurrected Christ. Not simply the Jesus who walked among men two thousand years ago, but the Jesus who, through all the power of the Godhead, raised Himself from death, from hell, from the snatching hands of all the demons of hell. And it is this power—His resurrected power, His victorious power—that now has taken up residence within my spirit.

Matthew 17:20 tells me that if I have faith as small as a mustard seed, I can say "Move!" to a mountain, and it will move. Why would I want to command a mountain to move, and what mountain? Well, I had a mountain of fear. I had a mountain of worry for my children and grandchildren. I had a mountain of pain and loss and sorrow. I had a mountain of regrets. I had a mountain of burdens too heavy to carry.

I cannot remove these mountains, because I don't have faith even as small as a mustard seed. I must have His faith.

A key word stood out to me in Galatians 2:20, which I clung to and which responded to my lack of faith. That word was "of"—the faith *of* the Son of God who loved me.

Now, with His faith and His resurrection power abiding in me, I can say to these mountains of fear, worry, pain, regrets, and burdens, "Be gone! Move into the midst of the sea!" and they will. And they did.

CHAPTER TWENTY-FOUR

He Knows His Soul Is Sick!

(Journal Entry 12-30-06)

Another Christmas; another new normal. This Christmas was surprisingly joyous. Joy in the midst of such turmoil and sorrow—what an amazing concept! Only God could do this.

The midnight prayer appointments were anointed times, as God continued to pour new things into me from every available source: Mike Wells, Beth Moore, David Wilkerson, Amy Carmichael, and Andrew Murray. Reading in Exodus, I felt Him draw near and show me new insight from His Word, all in the midst of much outside activity. At times, I felt as though I was in a supernatural dimension, watching from another place as events unfolded before me. The most amazing thing I noted at this time was that, whereas, for the past dozen or so years I had dragged myself through the holidays, wishing for them to be over, this year, for the first time in my adult life, I was thoroughly enjoying the holidays. I felt no pressure (having little or no money relieves an awful lot of pressure). But, the real difference was this year I had learned the most beautiful lesson: I learned truly and experientially that I had only one moment at a time in my life. I no longer had to bundle up all the upcoming moments and worry about or let them overwhelm me. I had one moment, and Jesus could give me as much or as little to do on any given day, and He could give me everything I needed to do it. So, I went through these very busy days with a supernatural calm and peace and, more important, joy! I loved decorating my house, I loved going to the festivities, I loved dropping everything and running over to Dane and Tasha's to watch them decorate their tree, I loved dressing up to go to the dinner parties and meeting leisurely at Starbuck's for four hours with my missionary friend Michelle, home for a visit. Surely, this was the "new thing" Jesus promised me during the terrible summer of 2005 (Isaiah 43:19 NKJV).

On December 23, Adam came with Jacob, and we all had a wonderful time visiting. We went downtown for dinner and then walked around the brightly lit courthouse square to view the light displays. Watching the pure excitement of the kids took all of us back to that magical time in our own childhoods. Later, we opened presents, and my sweet kids gave me a buttery soft calfskin Bible. Then John and I followed Adam and Jacob back to Phoenix for Christmas morning, a much quieter Christmas morning than any of us were accustomed to, and nice.

We spent the evening with family, sitting outside, around the firepit, in the mild Phoenix winter evening. I watched John as he struggled to adapt, struggled to enjoy himself, even though the inward restlessness was always urging him to rush away. I knew the loud family get-togethers were hard for him, too much sensory overload, so when I sensed he was ready to go, we left.

Back home in Prescott, another surprise awaited. The kids knew our old TV was on its last legs, so they found a nice year-old TV and had it hooked up for us when we got home. John, instead of being happy, seemed brusque, and when Dane asked him how he liked it, he was outright rude to him, barely acknowledging the gift. No matter how much intellectual understanding I had of this disease, it could still reach its tendrils around my trigger points and create a reflex reaction.

He didn't seem to understand why I was angry, but it was too late. With the disease now, it upset John to have me angry with him. The old behavior hadn't necessarily changed, but his ability to understand how it affected others had. He asked me to forgive him and became emotional, which always wrenched my heart to pieces. This time, however, he said something that stopped me dead in my tracks. He broke down, sobbing in my arms, and blurted out, "My soul is just so helpless!"

O God. O Jesus. He knows. He knows his soul is sick.

In the midst of all the chaos, confusion, and noise around me, my mind jolted to a stop in that moment, and I entered just briefly into John's world, where nothing made sense anymore. I gasped and caught my breath at the devastation—the ruins of lost memory, the crumbling of a life lived full and robust, now just stones, lying one upon another, no longer stacked neat and strong together. One here, one there.

December 28 arrived, the end of the six-month waiting period for disability payments to begin. Six months since our last income. The summer balloon check covered June through August and lasted longer than it should have. Our savings were being tapped in September, and even though the car needed repairs at least four times and the plumber had to be called on a holiday weekend, plus Christmas, Jesus gave us $1,200 from Dane and Tasha, $700 from my Wednesday Bible study ladies, and $1,400 from the small group. I was able to buy Christmas presents, not much, but enough. The cruse of oil never ran out; the wheat never failed. In fact, we still had $500 left over at the end of it all. I praise You Most High God, My Shepherd, my Redeemer.

CHAPTER TWENTY-FIVE

2007—O God, You Are My God

(Journal Entry 1-1-07)

O GOD, You are my God, earnestly will I seek You; my inner self thirsts for You, my flesh longs and is faint for You, in a dry and weary land where no water is. So I have looked upon You in the sanctuary to see Your power and Your glory. Because Your loving-kindness is better than life, my lips shall praise You. So will I bless You while I live; I will lift up my hands in Your name. My whole being shall be satisfied as with marrow and fatness; and my mouth shall praise You with joyful lips When I remember You upon my bed and meditate on You in the night watches. For You have been my help, and in the shadow of Your wings will I rejoice. My whole being follows hard after You and clings closely to You; Your right hand upholds me. (Psalm 63:1–8 AMP)

Finally, 2007 arrived—a year prophecy watchers have long anticipated. In the world, sabers are rattling: Iran, Iraq, Syria. Saudi Arabia, fearful of Iran; Jordan, fearful of Iraq. The very nations that line up against Israel in Ezekiel 38–39 have lined up. Again, those great cosmic upheavals match my own.

And He said, "My presence will go with you, and I will give you rest." (Exodus 33:14)

It felt like my commission for the year. The subject of His divinely appointed rest once again began moving around in my subconscious.

Around the middle of January, I got a call from an organization called Marketplace Chaplains. She said a friend had highly recommended me for a chaplain position. I decided I would go through doors as they opened, but I would not go forth on my own on this one.

We applied for assistance for John's health-care needs, and the long wait for that began. Becoming entangled in the maze of government webs was foreign to me. We found that we would be getting more than we anticipated from Social Security disability. Combined with our retirement disability, we would have enough to pay for John's insurance, but if we could qualify for temporary health-care assistance, that would help. Worry lurked around the corners of my mind, but I refused to pay attention to it. Jesus had proven His faithfulness, and He would do it all.

During this time, the doctor I wanted John to see called. He said would be giving a lecture at the hospital on dementia and invited me to come. I asked the receptionist about making an appointment now that John was covered, and she scheduled him for the following week. Another answer, one I had anxiously anticipated.

Something new seemed to be happening, and I barely wanted to think about it, much less mention it. For a few days, it felt like my old John was breaking through the mist. It could have been because his cousins Paul and David were coming for a visit, and he was beside himself with excitement. Whatever caused it, it felt good.

Walking down the hallway, I stopped him, gave him a big hug, and told him I loved him. He hugged me back and then followed me down the hall, still holding onto me like he used to do. Later, driving to the grocery store, I felt the strong presence of the Lord, and I suddenly blurted out, "Is he going to be healed?"

The next day, John helped me clean house and carried on a conversation, not shaky, or the repetitive weather report and endless questions, but with a strong and confident voice. Walking out of the bedroom, he blocked me from going out the door and teased me, like he used to do. I wrote this down, knowing it could be just a passing breakthrough, but strong in the knowledge that my God is huge and can do anything. Nothing is impossible to Him. As I watched God continue to minister to John's spirit while his soul was on hold, I often wondered if this was something like what happened to Nebuchadnezzar, a type of mental shutdown while God did a deep and mysterious work.

I silently prayed, "If there is anything to this, Lord, let it be a healing of his body, soul, and spirit. His soul, once so stubborn and proud, incapable of compassion, closed off emotionally, masked by too loud humor and laughing—could it have been damaged somehow along the way? So many secrets in his family—a dark side to all of it. I don't want to let my imagination run wild. I am willing for You to do anything—anything at all." The promise of August 2005—"'Do not remember the former things, Nor consider the things of old. Behold, I will do a new thing, Now it shall spring forth; Shall you not know it? I will even make a road in the wilderness And rivers in the desert'" (Isaiah 43:18, 19 NKJV)—seemed to return from time to time.

O God, You are my God ...

Meeting the new doctor, Dr. Matthies, I definitely knew he could take care of John's medical needs. My suspicions that he was a believer proved correct. He listened earnestly, paid close attention to everything I said, and asked pertinent questions, not just about the disease, but about John's spiritual life and his upbringing. With deep compassion, he asked me, "And how are you doing?" I fought back tears. None of the previous doctors had paid much attention to me, much less showed concern for how I was doing in the midst of John's illness.

He said he wanted to see John, and he also wanted me to write down all the things I had just related to him, which, of course, I had done all along and had a copy with me. He was the only doctor who had ever read my personal notes and observations. I left completely elated.

CHAPTER TWENTY-SIX

The Cousins

(Journal Entry 1-4-07)

And He said, 'My presence will go with you, and I will give you rest'(Exodus 33:13 NKJV).

John's cousins arrived on the afternoon of January 23, and as had always been the case, the volley of joking and laughter ensued. It felt so good to laugh out loud again. However, all the time they told the repertoire of funny stories, John was on disconnect, not connecting with the conversations or sharing in the joking and laughter. Paul and David noticed the dramatic changes. It was bittersweet.

Paul and I have always been close, like brother and sister, so we stayed up long after everyone else had gone to bed to talk. It was comforting to have someone to talk to about all of this, someone who knew John before.

Of course, it wouldn't have been a Beard visit without a mad drive. We took a drive to Strawberry and had lunch in the old lodge. We then went on to the Tonto Natural Bridge, which none of us had ever seen. It was spectacular, and the day was beautiful, crisp, and cool. Paul, David, and John hiked down into the ravine, where they could go under the bridge, while I waited on top and took pictures of them. I noticed that John was walking ahead alone. While they continued to another part of the trail, he came back up, anxious, impatient, wanting to get home.

When the others returned, we headed for home. But along the way, David spotted a dirt road leading to Fossil Creek, and we made a wild ride through seventeen miles of washboard desert road, over ridges and ice-covered shady spots, laughing all the while. John was not at all happy, however. He just wanted to go home. My old John would have been teasing the life out of me, as in the old days, I was the one like a horse heading for home, while he took off on remote roads to nowhere.

Finally back in Prescott, we met Dane and Tasha for dinner and then came home for the last night of our company's visit. Paul wanted me to download my pictures for him onto a CD, and I went in the office to do that, while they finished packing in the other room. John stood over me and hammered me with questions about what I was doing and why it wasn't working. Trying to concentrate, I asked him to just give me a minute; I had to figure something out. At that, he raised his voice, shouted at me to shut up, and raised his hand to hit me, stopping just inches from my face. Paul and David apparently didn't hear it, and I knew I had to keep my composure, but it drained everything out of me nevertheless.

The next day, after they left, he lost his temper again, this time over the doctors and the different things they were telling him. He picked up the bar stool and slammed it onto the floor. Afterward, he was apologetic of course, but I just was too tired to care. "Lord, please hear me," I prayed. "I'm just so tired of it all. I want this to be over."

Talking to Pat on the phone, I was able to voice my feelings, remembering when our dad was diagnosed with terminal cancer. We knew he was sick, but we had no idea how long he would live, and no one could tell us. At first, we busied ourselves with spending as much time as we could with him, packing in memories. Then, after a few months, he took a downturn and became bedridden, so we remained at the house for longer periods of time, because he seemed so close to going. He would even tell us that it would be that night, so we would sit up together on the great cedar deck he had built, crying and mourning. But the next morning, he would be awake and, at times, even better. This emotional roller coaster became nearly intolerable. When it seemed all our grieving had been done and it was time, death itself seemed to rise and mock us all, dragging on for another three months. The guilt of wanting to be free from the grip that impending death was holding us in, combined with the desperate need to get on with life and sitting, waiting, for endless hours in that house day after day, nearly destroyed us all.

So it was now with John's disease. It had already taken him, but there was no end in sight, no knowledge whatsoever of what the disease really was and what it would do next. The "third entity," as I had come to call it, was unknowable. It felt as if it had morphed again, and the violent side of it loomed over me, threatening to do me harm, while John himself looked at me with sweet helpless eyes, pleading for me not to be upset with him.

I found I could no longer watch anything frightening on TV, and I grew tense when I heard him walking from room to room, clomping loudly on our squeaky floor. I was on edge since Paul and David were here, my body felt taut; every fiber of my being seemed tightly strung like a bow. My head hurt, yet I still had to make all the phone calls to the health-care system that I had put off the week before. But, as had become my new normal, I woke the following Monday with no headache, lots of energy, and called everyone I needed to, all of whom were very kind. It appeared John would qualify for medical assistance.

Then there was the part of this disease that pointed its ugly finger at me when I was at my most vulnerable, accusing me of the what-ifs. One particular day at Pat's house, I heard an ominous voice declaring to me, "Every decision you have made has been wrong." Most kindhearted people would advise me to shut out these thoughts, resist them, but I always needed to examine them. In this case, I believed the Lord had some things for me to examine—not to accuse and condemn me; that was the work of the enemy.

One by one, the medical decisions I had made with and for John came to mind. I recalled scoffing initially at the first neurologist's suggestion that he was having seizures and wanting to medicate him for that. We already knew he had a colloid cyst in his brain, and both of us had decided that was causing other symptoms, so we rejected that possibility and requested to see the neurologists at Barrow. We may have moved in a wrong direction there. God gently allowed me to see that in the very beginning of this process, I had a great deal of pride and a great deal of contempt for the medical profession. I confessed this was true. I had learned by now that Jesus is not in the business of pointing the finger after the fact, but He lovingly reveals areas of our lives that are in bondage to pride or unbelief. He was not telling me that yes, John did have seizures and that I was responsible for preventing treatment. That would have been cruel; He just wanted me to see my pride in it.

I had also scoffed at the diagnosis of sleep apnea and had contempt for that doctor, because he was ready to stop at that place without further diagnosis. What was shown during the sleep test, however, was that John's oxygen saturation levels dropped radically as he slept, and he had not been getting enough oxygen. Whether that caused the dementia is anyone's guess. If so, it had been going on for a very long time, and there was no improvement in his symptoms after treatment.

During this time of examination, many of my decisions over the past couple of years were paraded before my mind. Have all of these decisions been wrong, Lord? Perhaps they have, and as I sit among the ruins of my life, what now?

I didn't answer those questions just then. I didn't have the emotional energy to think about all of it. What good would it do now, as nothing could change these things? The remainder of that week seemed to continue along this dreary, introspective path. I had made the appointment for John to see Dr. Matthies, and he was wonderful. He closely examined the PET scan that had been done the previous winter and asked if anyone had explained the findings. Of course, no one had. He said there were indications of a problem with the left frontal lobe, stating that seizure activity can cause damage to this lobe, as can low oxygen or hypoxia. He strongly urged John to get back on the CPAP sleep machine and oxygen.

Later, I looked up these things on the web and found that hypoxia is affected by altitude, which I knew affected John dramatically. The first real symptoms of confusion and memory loss occurred at the higher altitude of Big Lake in the summer of 2005.

I didn't even want to think about the possibility of seizure activity. In my research on left frontal lobe damage, I found there is an epilepsy connected to the left frontal cortex, and it can cause bradycardia and asystole (heart stoppage), which is exactly what John had experienced the summer of 2004. He had also had olfactory aura, which is associated with it. There had been no further indications of seizures, and when I asked John's cardiologist about it, he said that the pacemaker had resolved all of those issues.

Will I ever know the answers to these things? I asked myself. *Am I supposed to know?* I could not rest as long as there was the slightest possibility that the answers lay out there somewhere. But, God was not giving me those answers, and in the process, He was again telling me there was a supernatural rest He was trying to work into me, a supernatural peace only waiting can produce.

Later in the night watch, I rose from my bed, which often felt like my worst enemy, and sat alone in front of my large living room window, looking out at the stars and sky. It was all so huge; God is so huge. I put on my iPod and listened in the dark to Fernando Ortega softly singing the words to my life verse:

O God you are my God.

Peace returned.

CHAPTER TWENTY-SEVEN

Letting Go of Old Memories/Creating New Ones

(Journal Entry 2/10/07)

Following the leading I sensed from the Lord about doing more of the things John enjoys, after he expressed an interest in taking a drive to Wickenberg, we took a day trip; the first one in a long while.

I had been avoiding taking day trips, as I dreaded the transition from our old way of doing things—John "mad-driving," taking us on crazy adventures, not knowing where they would lead, laughing at his jokes, and loving every minute of it. We could take off into unknown territory, because of John's uncanny sense of direction; he never got lost, no matter how far off the beaten path we were. I, on the other hand, got lost driving in my own city. So, for me to take over this part of our lives seemed pretty foreboding. However, as it turned out, John no longer wanted to go off the beaten path at all. Once he fixed his mind on a destination or something he wanted to do, there was nothing along the way that interested him.

As we drove the familiar road into Skull Valley and passed our favorite country store, he asked if we hadn't stopped there before. I reminded him that we always stopped there for the pickled eggs and asked if he wanted to stop there now. "Oh no, no, let's just get to Wickenberg." His mind was set. On this trip, I kept hearing in my heart that now-familiar verse, "Forget the former things" (Isaiah 43:18 NKJV), and remembered what Diane had suggested recently: that maybe God wanted me to say goodbye to my old memories, my memories of the old John. So, unlike a year ago, when John and I made this trip and I fought back the tears along every familiar landmark, I now consciously and deliberately surrendered the old for the new.

It was a perfectly wonderful day. John enjoyed it so much. We ate at a favorite restaurant, which he didn't remember, but he loved it. He kept grabbing my hand at the table, and with eyes filled with tears, he repeated again and again, "I'm so glad we did this." Yes, I decided, we would do it more often, albeit with me at the wheel, a decidedly non-mad driver.

Valentine's Day was very sweet, bittersweet. John and I went to a new restaurant that he enjoyed, and he talked about it for the rest of the day. Those things seemed to mean so much to him.

I finally heard from the health-care program, and they were waiting to hear how much John's state retirement's final check would be now that we were getting Social Security. After talking to a representative from the retirement office, I was blown away. We would be getting a combined income of $700 more per month than we did while John was employed! Whether or not we qualified for the health care, we would be able to afford insurance for John. Amazing.

Later, I learned John qualified for the health care, for which we would be paying $240 a month. Again, God had provided. It felt like a great hurdle had been removed—after two years of waiting.

I also met with a social worker who specialized in dementia, and she was a wealth of information. It was one of those unmistakable God-sent events. She had plain, commonsense counsel, not New Age happy talk. She gave me guidelines and instructions—people to contact, ideas to keep John busy, how to talk to and relate to him, and what to look for in the future. One of the most important things she did was to give me "permission" to stop trying to find the cause or the cure. She advised me to accept it and learn to live with it. She told me how to live in his moments, listen to what he says, and never try to argue or reason with him. Her exact words: "It is unreasonable to try to reason with an unreasonable person." These were things I already knew, but now it was time to put them into practice.

She also warned me that he would probably live only a maximum of six years after symptoms appeared, and more likely only four because of his age. At this point, we were into year three. She also emphatically stated that for some reason surgery could cause dementia to escalate, which made me question the upcoming hernia surgery.

A wonderful sermon that following weekend dovetailed perfectly with all I had been hearing from God. Brokenness: truly the message for the hour. The text was from Psalm 66:10–12: "For You, O God, have tested us; You have refined us as silver is refined. You brought us into the net; You laid affliction on our backs. You have caused men to ride over our heads; We went through fire and through water; But You brought us out to rich fulfillment" (NKJV).

It was God who tested us, who refined us as silver, who brought us into the net. He laid the affliction on our backs and caused men to ride over our heads. But it was also God who brought us out to rich fulfillment. That was the promise: one day He would bring me out into rich fulfillment.

My Wednesday night Bible study had burgeoned from ten to fifteen regulars to thirty. We had been doing a Beth Moore study on Daniel, and all of our lives were being greatly impacted by it. My heart loved these ladies so much. They filled my life with so much joy.

The man who had recommended me for the chaplain position invited me to lunch at the lovely Peacock Room at the old Hassayampa Inn, where he gave me sound counsel on financial matters. At the end of our lunch, he and his wife presented me with an envelope containing a check for $500. God was already restoring the years the locust had eaten in my life. I was humbled and awed.

At small group later that week, Guy asked a few of us to give our testimonies, and by the end of the evening, we were all in tears with an everlasting bond formed between us. I passionately loved the way God was creating His tapestry of lives, weaving us all together—all of our lives building upon the other, combining with each other, mingling the colors and textures into a lovely and glorious picture.

I wondered how these various tapestries looked to Him from above— some woven into lovely pastoral scenes, sheep lying in a pasture with the Shepherd nearby, watching over; some in places of persecution, woven into glorious deeply saturated hues of reds and golds, sunsets and storms. And I wondered what the tapestry He was weaving of my life would look like in the end. It was His picture. He could add to it or take away from it as He pleased, but it was His.

CHAPTER TWENTY-EIGHT

Three Steps Forward, Two Steps Back

(Journal Entry 3-18-07 to 3-20-07)

Three steps forward,; two backward:

Two steps backward. Another bout with the doctors and health-care coverage. John's hernia needed to be removed, but this time I noticed a complete change in how this all affected me, compared to a year ago. Again, I was reminded of the "rest" God was teaching me. Resting is waiting without worry. After many phone calls and the usual hassles, John was scheduled to see the gastroenterologist. In the meantime, I had tried to get him in to see Dr. Matthies, but they weren't able to take the coverage we had, so that came to a dead end.

Three steps forward. Amazingly, however, I got a packet from Marketplace Chaplains that stated I had been hired. God is amazing. The twists and turns my life had taken over the past few years I would never have imagined. Only He knew where He was taking me. Only He knew how this story would end.

Two steps backward. The next day, John, who had began going online to check our bank account, announced from the office that we had $45 in our checking account. I was only half listening and then it struck me: there should be much more than that; the bills had not been paid. I rushed in to check my accounts, got online, and found a draft had been written on our account that had wiped us out. I printed out the draft, and it seemed to be an electronic check with our account number, but it didn't look like one of our checks. I grabbed everything and rushed to the bank. They froze our accounts, canceled our debit cards, and opened a new account right away. The customer service rep told me it wasn't safe to write checks any longer. Apparently, someone had gotten hold of one of our checks and used the routing numbers. A reminder that the world we live in isn't safe, outside of Jesus.

Three steps forward. All of this happened just before I was to teach, and again, I discovered to my amazement that I was very calm throughout the ordeal and went on to Bible study in perfect peace.

Two steps backward. The following Monday, a letter came about our disability retirement. Because we were now getting Social Security, we were expected to pay back two months' retirement benefits. I had just begun replenishing my savings and that would clean it out. I had twenty days to repay over $2,000. John got the letter before I could see it, and he went into sensory overload, firing questions, demanding to know what was going on, frustrated, threatening to call—all before I could look at the letter.

When I finally got to see the letter myself, I still couldn't concentrate because of his rapid-fire volley of questions. I left and drove to Pat's house to think this through. A torrential downpour of discouragement and disappointment crashed in on me, and I let go of the anchor and let it carry me off, succumbing to hopelessness and even unbelief. I came home with unresolved feelings of despair.

Adam called. I talked to him, and he was very encouraging as always, praying a wonderful prayer. Then Dane called, and I told him about it, half joking that life wasn't fair, in so many words, not all of them printable. He turned the entire event into a joke, teasing me about my lack of faith and his words got me laughing. "So Mom, you said you wanted to learn how to give God more, so the Bible says to give to whoever asks. If the government is asking, give it to them!" Of course! How simple.

Mike Wells writes that what you are in your worst moment is what you really are. This is why the flesh cannot ever really change: it is the *flesh* after all. In my worst moment, the same things surfaced—unbelief, lack of trust.

Not being able to trust seemed to be a very big issue between God and I, and He was relentlessly after this issue. Over the next few days, I asked Him to open this wound and heal it from the inside out. He did, taking me back to events in my own childhood that led to my inability to trust or to feel that anyone could trust me. My problem was not simply that I didn't trust anyone, not even God, but that I never felt that others—God in particular—could trust me. It went back to an old feeling that He was always trying to catch me, always setting traps for me to fail, to prove that

I will always fail. This was directly related to a specific event in my life, and on this day, He allowed that event to play through my mind like a movie. As I was going through this intensive "therapy" session, I was reading a devotional that began:

> And we know that all things work together for good to those who love God, to those who are the called according to His purpose. (Romans 8:28 NKJV)

> The only forgiveness that is worth anything is that which makes it possible for us to forgive ourselves. It is one thing to say "God forgives." It is another to forgive ourselves. (Kendall, R.T. *A Treasury of Wisdom.* Uhrichsville, OH: Barbour Publishing, 1998, p. 90.)

I'm not going back there again, Lord. I feel like I have been down that road again and again. Jesus, please heal this thing, whatever it is.

> What is God saying to you? … Our gracious God comes from behind to shape your past so that, if you will believe Him and give Him time, you will come to see that His hand was with you even at your worst moment. (Ibid.)

This was a "worst moment," and when I saw it, I asked Him, "Where were you when this happened? I need to see You in this picture."

Three steps forward. He showed me. He showed me my mother, her unconditional love, her modeling of forgiveness and love. No matter what I did, she still trusted me; she modeled Jesus. It was a dramatic and profound thing God did, throughout my entire life since then, working even that event for good, just as He promised. Now, because of this, I was able to relate to the people God sent to me to offer His comfort and encouragement, and He alone gets the glory.

> Oh the relief I feel to know that God was with me in my worst moment! But this is the sovereign grace of God. Only a God like that can do it. He can shape your past and take your worst moment and, in time, so redeem your past that you can look back and not wish to change anything. This is the God of the Bible. (Ibid.)

I now felt a healing. I felt the peace of God return, my prayers returned, His presence was near. The enemy made one last attempt at robbing my peace as our Social Security check was late, lost in the mail somewhere. But it was too late. God had already healed my mind and heart, and the power of the enemy had been destroyed.

The training for the chaplain position was next on the agenda, and on the following day, we went to Meadowpark Care Center, where we would serve. Another female chaplain and I would serve the women employees, and a local pastor would serve the men. We were just introduced that first day, but after the meeting, several Hispanic women rushed right over to meet me. I met with one of them that day and prayed with her. She was very appreciative. I wanted to set her up for further counseling with a Spanish-speaking counselor and discovered from a friend in our outreach ministry that Juan Garcia, a wonderful pastor of the Spanish-speaking ministry at my church, might be able to help. I contacted him, and he became a true resource for these women. Within a short time, several of them were meeting with him and attending church. God brought the harvest after the "humblings," as Beth Moore taught.

The thing about these humblings is that they are ongoing. There is not a single event where one surrenders it all, a great harvest takes place, and all the trials are over. It seems more like a monthly, or even weekly, humbling followed by a harvest, a humbling, and another harvest. Why had I always thought that it was a one-time deal? I had learned in the abiding life that before I can really get hold of this teaching, I had so much to *unlearn*, so many "untrue truths" lurking in my mind. When we take *a* truth and make it *the* truth, it can become an *untruth*.

The week following the humblings was filled with harvests. God brought many women into my path all week, all broken, discouraged, disappointed.

John's surgery was finally scheduled. I was uneasy about the effects of the anesthesia, but it actually went very well. His oxygen saturation levels kept dropping, but no one seemed too worried about it. When I went in to see him in post-op, he was sitting up, drinking juice, and bright and chipper, as though this time the anesthesia had the reverse effect. He looked back to normal, talking about normal things and even joking a bit with Linda. At home, he continued this way. The next morning, he was up early and fixing his breakfast—not pacing, not repeating things, not giving me a weather report. I had learned, however, not to let my emotions get on the roller coaster of these ups and downs, and within a few days, he was back to being somber and subdued. But, later in the week, he did something the old John used to do: walking past me, he affectionately grabbed my toes, one by one, pulling them. Later that evening, he turned and looked at me, smiled, and made kissing sounds. These familiar little things couples do without thinking broke through from time to time, and it made me homesick for my John.

It came time for the commissioning for the chaplaincy, which was to take place at church. There was a bittersweetness to it. Suddenly, I didn't want to do this ministry. Suddenly, it felt too much like moving on without John. All the years of longing to do ministry with him, and now, this seemed so final. Officially, it was now ministry as one, without my husband.

CHAPTER TWENTY-NINE

Crazy-Making!

(Journal Entry 5/4/07)

What schizophrenia this disease creates! Crazy-making behavior (not for John, but for me). I sometimes feel that if it were not for You, Jesus, I would become what the enemy of my soul would so like for me to be—just put into that pit, finally, and sealed over. Thanks be to You, oh Lord, my God, that You will hold me and not allow the enemy to win.

On Monday, I was filled with grief, compassion, and love for John. Throughout the week, I moved back and forth between waking with a terrible headache and fatigue to waking filled with energy. Somehow, I managed to get through many meetings, but along the way, John suddenly announced to me that there was nothing wrong with him. He, "only had a sleep problem, that was all," maybe a "little problem" with his memory and, of course, the old arrow that always found its mark: "You are just making this all up!"

So, I went again from that place of deep grieving, begging God not to take him from me, to John himself taking on the very lie of the enemy, plunging me back to old baggage. Many reading this may wonder why these old arrows still found a place to lodge, why didn't this writer ever get it that her husband has dementia, that he can't help what he is doing and saying? I agree. However, these were old marriage issues, long unresolved, and even though he was not in his right mind, his words were the same. Those words were baggage, and that baggage consisted of a lot of wonderful memories intermingled with some very unhappy ones. The happy times were happy as long as I knew my place, and that place was as John's cute little wife who adored him but was never allowed to have serious conversations about deeper issues. My place was the constant conditioning that John was always right. If there was a problem, it must be my problem, because John couldn't be wrong; he simply could not comprehend himself as being wrong.

So now, even though I knew intellectually he was not in control of what he said, emotionally, the message still got to me: "I *am* making this all up, there can't be anything wrong with him, it must be me." I knew it must have been terribly difficult for John to see me in control of his life. He was always in control of everything. I think in some ways, he had to lash out at me to feel he had regained some control. He had always taken care of me, and he was wonderful at that. He never let me take care of him, though, never let me cook, do his laundry, or do anything for him. Now that I had been forced against my will (and his) to take over so many of the things he had always done, the transition and shifting of all of the dynamics in our relationship became very complicated.

Driving to a meeting the next day, I felt God release me emotionally from my role as John's caretaker. Not from the caretaking, but from the emotional toll of it. I had no guidebook for this disease; what worked for one person may not work for the other. I found myself calling it a "damning" disease. It is confusing, sometimes evil, and it will—if you allow it to—drive a sane person completely insane.

> Thank You, Jesus. Now, this moment, right now, I yield John and myself into Your caretaking. You are the caretaker for both of us. You have allowed this disease into our lives and You have a plan and a purpose for it. Just as You healed me from the control issues You recently revealed to me, so now You are healing me and setting me free from this thing that John wields over me. Only You are in control of my emotions.

For my birthday, John seemed like his old self, planning a nice steak dinner for me, bustling around in the kitchen, which he hadn't done in a long while, cooking up a storm. But it was his card to me that hit me the hardest. The little verse inside mentioned specifically taking care of him when he was sick. He had obviously carefully picked out this card, and again, my heart was carried away in a bittersweet melody. The words sweet and beautiful, the emotions in a minor key, tinged with sadness.

It was now warm enough to open windows at night. When I awoke, I could hear the chirping of the birds and feel the cool air wafting over my bed, turning my mind instantly to a transfixed thanksgiving to God. As I sang praise to Him, inviting Him into my day, He was faithful to go before me and give me His peace. Each day, no matter how exhausted I fell into bed the night before, I woke up in peace. And the icing on the cake—He sent a nice rain that week.

The best part was that the cruse of oil did not run out in spite of mounds of unbudgeted expenses. John had bought a ticket to fly to Maryland; we had numerous birthdays and dinners and many other expenses. Yet, at the end of May, I had money to spare. I had even made a mistake and paid my RV payment twice for May, and there was still a surplus. Who can understand the ways of God?

The following week, my friend Diane invited me to drive down to Tucson with her and Guy for the Michael Wells conference. Pat was thrilled that I would be staying with her. So, that weekend was a time of fellowship, talking about the Lord, and meeting with Mike Wells. I felt as though I already knew him, so much of the abiding life teaching had been molded into my experience.

Once again, the dementia invaded. As Pat was showing me her new computer sound system, she put in an old CD of Marc Cohn, a favorite artist of mine and John's. Then the song "True Companion" came on—a tune John had turned into an "our song" back in the early 1990s. Out of nowhere, hearing the first strains of the melody and words, tears and memories and grief shot through me like a hot iron. I nearly burst out in uncontrollable sobbing. I had to ask her to turn it off. I remembered the first time we had heard the song: John was so moved by it that he held me and cried. Now, hearing it brought back a deep well of loneliness for John, and all I could say was, "I was loved by that man."

Later, back at home and reflecting on all of that, I realized that going alone to the conference, feeling like a widow, and coming home to John, who was not really here, the sadness of it all was mind-boggling. Now, Jesus was asking to be my all—to completely replace John—to have our special songs and memories and moments. "When you come into the Promised Land, build an altar of stones, washed white with lime and offer peace offerings and eat and rejoice there" (Deuteronomy 4:7 my paraphrase). I am crossing over Jordan, it seems. I have not yet crossed over, but my feet are getting wet.

CHAPTER THIRTY

Summer at Last

(Journal Entry 5/31.07)

Last day of May. Summer is here at last, green leaves,
windows open, that marvelous cool breeze brushing over me
in my bed at night and the chorus and symphony of music in
the early morning by His creation is finally back.

God created so many different birds to sing. There was that mournful
dove, reminding me of Jeremiah lamenting. Sometimes I mourned
with them. Finches chattered back and forth to each other, never running
out of conversation. The grackles, an annoying bird and a nest robber,
sent a tropical sound through the air, reminding me of far-off places.
Others—not identifiable to me—also sang their own songs. All of these
creatures sang at once—different melodies, songs, keys, words—yet they
all blended together in one choir that spoke to me of the sons of God
rejoicing at creation.

Hearing those melodies transported me back to my childhood in the
large bedroom in our little farm on Roger Road, three of our beds lined
up in a row, venetian blind–covered windows on every wall allowing the
room to be washed with sunlight every morning. Lying in bed in the early
morning and hearing the doves across the alfalfa fields. I thought they
were owls that lived at the Douglas's big old farmhouse, surrounded by
cottonwoods and tamarisk trees.

Old memories flooded my mind: memories of playing long hours in
the cottonwood-lined irrigation ditches of Roger Road, building forts
together with the gang of kids—Peter, Lynn, Ellie, and the others. We

were always in awe of the teenage boys with their "waterfall haircuts," blue jeans, white T-shirts, and hotrods.

I loved those summers. Waking up early now to the sound of those doves, for just a moment, everything felt safe again. I mourned the loss of innocence—not merely my own, but the innocence of the time in which I grew up. If one word could describe those years, it would have to be "safe." But, the world no longer felt safe. Not for us, not for our children. There is safety only in Christ.

John had taken it on himself to make airline reservations to visit his family in Maryland. I knew I must let him go, although I was not at peace about his return trip, since he would have to change planes in Houston. I put out a fleece to the Lord that if I could get a ticket for a reasonable price and get on his return flight, I would fly out for the last week of his visit. It did work out, so I bought my ticket for July 24.

We managed to get in one camping trip with Dane and the grandkids before they closed all the forests because of drought and fire danger. It was really wonderful. We went back to Whitehorse, where we could sit on the lake. The kids played nonstop, searching for crawdads and treasures along the lake. Dane and I sat up late every evening to watch the fire die down and talk.

Watching John, I could see his behavior was similar to that of my five-year-old grandson. Every suggestion was met with an argument, every direction answered with "why?" every attempt to assist met with "I can do it!" I was living with a fifty-eight-year-old five-year old.

Back home, the news for the past few months had centered on the increase of lawlessness in our country. These things weighed on me and threatened to take me to the pit. My soul was vexed; discouragement loomed over me. Yet somehow, I found myself writing at 2:00 a.m., as a spirit of intercession came over me and words flowed from me almost involuntarily:

> Lord Jesus, I am weak—thank You that Your strength is perfected in my weakness. I fail and falter—thank You that Your love never fails. I cannot abide in You, but Your love abides forever. I can't love John with perfect love, but You love Him with the love of Calvary; I may never see the changes I so long to see in all of those I pray for, but You are faithful and You never fail and You will do it.

I will likely lose John to this brain disease, but You set up kings and take kings down, and You are working humility and love into his heart, even in the midst of this brain disease. Glory belongs to You, Most High God.

The world is dying—lawlessness abounds, but You have overcome the world. We don't have enough money this month, but You feed the sparrows and clothe the lilies, and we are of much more value to You than they. You have overcome the world and because of that, I can boldly say that I can overcome all these things by the blood of the Lamb and the word of my testimony, and I do not love my life even unto death.

I can boldly declare that my Lord and Savior Jesus Christ disarmed rulers and authorities, making a public spectacle of them and triumphing over them at the cross; therefore, these rulers and authorities having assignment against me, my husband, and sons are disarmed and defeated by the cross. "Therefore I will look to the LORD, I will wait for the God of my salvation. My God will hear me! Do not rejoice over me, oh my enemy. When I fall I will arise. When I sit in darkness, the LORD will be a light to me." (Micah 7:7–8 NKJV)

Now unto him that is able to keep you from falling, and to present you faultless before the presence of his glory with exceeding joy, To the only wise God our Saviour, be glory and majesty, dominion and power, both now and ever. Amen. (Jude: 24, 25)

CHAPTER THIRTY-ONE

The Relentless Pace of Life

(Journal Entry 6-30-07)

I will be there with you; I will give you rest.

June burst onto the scene without so much as a pause for rest or reflection. Dane and Tasha moved, and I took care of the kids for five days. After that week, I found myself sitting in the presence of the Lord in the early morning, very tired. Reading in my devotional on the Song of Solomon, Jesus spoke softly and tenderly to my heart:

> "When you are tired dear Christian, do you ever just sit in His presence, briefly read a word from His lips such as Psalm 23 and then lay back and rest in those promises right there and then? He will refresh you. It is not a time for study. (Psalm 48–49)

> "My love, my Bride, look at Me, look into My eyes. Listen to my voice! No matter what the enemy will bring against you; no matter how intense the problems and difficulties may be, look my darling Bride, I have already conquered them!

> "I will be there with you when you face the mountains of fear, doubt, depression, failure and loss which will try to rob you of peace joy and contentment ... I will be with you on the hills of irritation, mental tiredness, physical

weakness and family difficulties … Just be patient and wait. My Bridegroom love will sustain you through the storms." (Shoshannah, Esher, *I Love You With All My Heart, Always, Jesus.* Tucson, AZ: Self-published, www.songofsolomondevotional.com, p. 48)

My nephew Paul and his family had now moved to Prescott, down the street from me. Paul went to work for Dane, and many new things seemed to be in store, as well as new times of training for this family. I had a sense that a new season was coming—a season of growth among those who had slacked off. But, there was also the foreboding that this season would not come without cost.

There were two attempted terrorist attacks in London and Scotland, putting everything on high alert again. John would be flying to Maryland on July 10, and I feared the heightened security at the airport would cause more anxiety in him if he were asked to step aside for further scrutiny. But again, I had to leave this with Jesus. John hadn't flown by himself since the summer of 2005, when his symptoms had just begun to manifest. I knew he could erupt abruptly, as I had witnessed once again while going through the usual health-care maze of getting him approved for oxygen for his CPAP machine.

July had been very hot; tempers were hot as well. A friend I had been discipling was calling a lot, and I noticed this made John tense. In the space of about fifteen minutes one afternoon, one of those eruptions hit without warning. I was irritated with the oxygen dilemma, and John, mistaking this as irritation with him, suddenly went into a flash of anger, raising a clinched fist to my face, stopping, I believe, by the hand of an angel. Cold fear enveloped me, and I took advantage of having to go meet a friend to get away from him.

While sitting at Coco's with my friend, John came in and stood over our table, trying to apologize. I took him outside, where he broke down. It was awful. I realized then that I could not continue to meet with women like this, as things at home were simply too stressful. I was having difficulty separating my home life from this ministry.

Yet, somehow, life continued on.

Adam got married to a very sweet and loving woman, Jeniece, on July 7. It was an emotion-filled week. I was tired from having company the previous week and worried about John leaving three days later. Pete, the boys' dad, was at the wedding, which always brought up a lot of pain for me. But during the ceremony, I somehow gained new strength as Jesus always provides when I need it most.

CHAPTER THIRTY-TWO

The Floodgates Open

(Journal Entry 7/10/07)

I just dropped John off for the airport. Watching him in the van, like a child waving and waving, he did something he would have done years ago, something to make me laugh. For just a brief second I flashed back to my trip to Maryland in May of 1985. As I was leaving on the tram to the plane watching John, and crying, he continued to make signs with his hands indicating something funny and I kept having to laugh instead of cry. He always made me laugh.

After dropping him off I cried all the way home. I should say I wailed all the way home, because that is what it was. The floodgates were now opened; I hadn't cried in a very long time.

Jesus spoke very tenderly to me early the next morning

From the shadow of the cross, He said of you:

"I pray for them. I am not praying for the world, but for those You have given me, for they are yours. All I have is Yours, and all You have is mine. And glory has come to me through them." (John 17: 9–10 NIV)

O Lord, my God, I hear You.

Reading from Amy Carmichael's little devotional, she wrote of her soul entering into the iron fetters:

Would I merely endure it, praying for the grace not to make too much over my poor circumstances? Or, would my soul willingly enter into the "iron" of this new and difficult experience?

There could be only one answer to that…Philippians 1:13—"My bonds in Christ"—I knew that all was well indeed …

So there could be nothing but peaceful acceptance. And when one accepts, then all that is included in the thing is accepted too—in my case, the helplessness, the limitations, the disappointments of hope deferred, the suffering.

I now know this is important in keeping our spiritual "atmosphere" clear. For if we let even the fugitive wisp of a cloud float across our sky (in the form of a wish—that is, a wish that things were different!) then the whole sweet blue of our spirit is swiftly overcast.

But if we refuse that wisp of cloud … ! If we look up and meet the love of the Lord that shines down on us, and say to Him about that particular detail of the trial "Dear Lord, yes."

Then, in one bright moment, our sky is blue again.

Lord, give me the grace to say "Yes" today—yes to the helplessness, the limitations, the disappointments of hope deferred, the suffering. (Carmichael, Amy. *You Are My Hiding Place*. Minneapolis, MN: Bethany House Publishers, 1991, pp. 92, 93)

Speaking to me on so many levels, I personalized this in my journal:

Hold me Jesus. I cannot do this.

CHAPTER THIRTY-THREE

A Respite and a New Time of Training

(Journal Entry 7/12/07)

It is becoming clear to me that this two week respite is not merely a time for rest from John's disease—which permeates every corner of the house—but a new time of training. Amen.

After spending the first day crying almost uncontrollably, the second day alone seemed glorious. I took an early morning walk before the heat descended; the breeze was cool, and I walked listening to music. Then, I sat on my back deck, which overlooks the distant hills, and praised God for His beautiful creation. I took on a couple of big house projects—which Dane and Paul had to finish. Their crazy dialogue, however, also provided much entertainment for me.

The next morning, once again sitting in my prayer corner and listening to the family of quail who had taken up residence in my front yard, I read in Judges 8:4 of Gideon's army in pursuit of the Midianites. It said that they were, "exhausted but still in pursuit," and I heard the faintest whispering of the Lord concerning the constant strain of this emotional battle I live in—the battle with the army of dementia. Just because John was not here did not mean I simply lay down and quit everything and everyone. I realized that I coveted my time alone, which was fine, but I also needed to keep an open line with friends and family.

In Psalm 56, David writes, "You number my wanderings" (Psalm 56:8 NKJV), and even the slightest "wandering" off this path of abiding in Him into a side eddy of self-pity or self-absorption could not go unchecked. He *gives* His beloved rest. I am not to demand it; I am not to hoard it. It is His rest, and He would give it as He saw fit.

Amy Carmichael's devotional completed the instruction:

> "And what we will be has not yet been made known" (1 John 3:2).
>
> Through these months, acceptance has been a word of liberty and victory and peace to me. But it has never meant acquiescence in illness, as though evil circumstances were from Him who delights to deck His servants with health.
>
> "But He knows the way that I take; when He has tested me, I will come forth as gold" (Job 23:10).
>
> " [All kinds of trials come] So that your faith—of greater worth than gold, which perishes, even though tried by fire—may be proved genuine" (1 Peter 1:7).
>
> My Father, if You are working into me some traits I would not have chosen to work on myself (for example patience!), then I ask for Your grace to carry me through. Purify me of everything but perfect acceptance in you. (Ibid., p. 95)

The second week into my respite, I spoke to John's cousin Paul, who filled me in on events in Maryland. They were taking John to his cousin David's that Friday, and he was to stay the weekend there. However, he had settled into his cousin Linn's house and didn't want to leave. Julie called it "nesting." Paul tried to persuade him but with no success. Julie finally came over, and with her behavioral training, she managed to nudge him out of the house. This was absolutely not in John's character; he loved to visit and stay with all his cousins. I felt that maybe he was not doing well, certainly not because of anything anyone was doing there, but because of some apparent disorientation taking place.

The two weeks went fast. Another thing became clear to me during this time. When all was said and done, I realized that I did not want to be alone. Despite all the time I spent longing for time alone, I realized now that too much time alone is just lonely. As difficult as it was now with John,

I missed him terribly. That first day alone, I felt the whole brunt that his dying would bring, and my grief was inconsolable.

CHAPTER THIRTY-FOUR

Maryland: A Blessed Respite

(Journal Entry 7-22-07)

Old-fashioned Southern hospitality and graciousness. What a respite. John seemed vastly improved in Maryland with his family; should I try to move him there for these last years of his life?

On Monday, I cleaned the house and left for Phoenix. Just prior to landing, I was fighting back tears. Somewhere inside, I was expecting to meet my old John, remembering how over twenty years ago, I had made this flight to see the man who had become my soul mate in such a short time. I was wishing with all my heart that it would be the strong and competent John standing there, waiting for me at the airport. I had to keep reminding myself that he was not there anymore. Memories are stubborn that way.

Arriving in Baltimore, I could see John and Paul ahead, John searching the crowd to find me. When he saw me, his face crumpled, and he began crying. Paul later told me he felt John came alive after I got there, and I think he did.

Waking up that first morning at Aunt Doris's warm and welcoming home, I felt a stirring within, an intense desire to see John healed. I am not sure I can adequately define my emotions, but what I said to the Lord was, "I have been double-minded. One minute I am asking You to heal my husband and the next I am asking You to take him home because I want this to be over. Now, my heart and my mind are in agreement, and I am going to begin asking You to heal him. I don't know what Your will is. So not knowing, I'm just going to begin fervent effectual prayers that You will heal him." I felt tremendous peace in praying this.

The rest of my stay was glorious, even anointed. The weather was cool, humid but not unbearable. Doris and I loved to sit on the porch in our pajamas and drink our morning coffee, talking for a long time about the Lord. John's longtime friend Darrell came from Alexandria the day after I arrived, and Doris fixed us a nice lunch. She had bought a bushel of peaches, which I ate to my heart's content. Later, we took Darrell over to Linn's, who had graciously offered to put him up for the night. If there was a word to describe this family, it was true Southern hospitality—old South graciousness.

As for John, he seemed to be showing signs of actual improvement. On Thursday, we went to our old favorite places to shop. John was looking intently for a "Barn Star" for our house since so many houses there had them. Then, we went to the outlet stores, where he seemed excited again to buy some clothes. It was good to see him with his old excitement and enjoying himself so much. All day he broke into big grins and told me over and over how glad he was to be able to do that. I was filled with a new love for him. God was doing something in my heart there, and it felt good; it felt right to be here.

Friday, we went to David and Kathy's and stayed the night so that they could take us on a leisurely canoe trip down the Potomac the next day. Their house was nestled in the deep woods, near the old Antietam battleground. I got up early in the morning and watched as several deer grazed in their yard. The canoe trip was amazing, slow and leisurely, just like the river itself. At one point, a bald eagle flew directly overhead, one of those moments when God seemed to be speaking His peace to me, carrying my soul up on those great wings, and indeed, I was surrounded by His peace in this place.

Back in Hagerstown that evening, Doris had a big family gathering with a spread of wonderful "steamers," fresh corn on the cob, peach pie, and several side dishes, all lovingly made from scratch.

Sunday we rested, got our things washed and packed, and in the afternoon, went to Paul and Bobbi's for another dinner, spread out on long tables on a wide green lawn under a canopy of tall trees. A rainstorm blew in. Paul put up his Ezy-up canopy, and we continued to eat outside, while the rain poured all around us.

Back in the living room later, their daughter Beca played the piano and sang some Christian songs for us. Then, she and Paul played some together. She also played a fiddle, and together, they delighted us with Irish jigs. Sitting there, watching, I thought, *I could live here; these people are as much family to me as my own.*

Monday came all too soon, and it was time to leave for home. It had been an anointed trip—full of surprises from the Lord. Twice, Paul got John to laugh out loud, his old belly laugh that I hadn't heard in at least three years. Linn also got him to laugh, and he seemed to smile the entire time we were there. He was almost giddy when shopping. He seemed so happy, so at peace, not restless and pacing. I wondered if it might be possible for us to move there for a short time, but there were so many cumbersome details that would have to be worked out.

The trip home went well, but John seemed subdued, almost worried. At home, I mentioned to him how happy he seemed when we were there and wondered if he might like to go back for a longer time. What he said took me by surprise. With complete cognizance, he looked straight into my eyes and said, "I didn't tell you this before I left, but when I made plans to go to Maryland, I knew I had to go, because I knew it would be the last time I would ever go back. I will not be making any more trips back there again." Then he hugged me and told me he loved me and wanted to be here with me. I cried. I asked him what he meant, why he thought he would never go back, but that was all he would share.

Oh God, what does this mean? Have You given him insight into his future? Is he going to die? Does he know that his mind will continue to descend into darkness? What am I to make of this new revelation?

Later, in my prayer closet, I sensed strongly that now was the time to leave off all my outside activities and devote myself only to John. God had been doing a miracle in my heart for the past three weeks, changing my attitudes, giving me instructions. I didn't know where any of this was going now, but I was enveloped in such calm and peace. I didn't even need to ask for it; it was given to me supernaturally. Over and over, Jesus confirmed to me that, at least for a season, I was to devote myself and my time to John.

It began to gel in my mind what I was to continue to do and what to stop. The Wednesday night Bible study could continue, since John also attended a Bible study on that night. All of the one-to-one discipleship would have to stop, however, as much for me as for John. I felt unable to listen to other's problems for this period, even though I had done it the previous year with such joy. The question God had asked me in the summer of 2005, "Will you lay it all down for Me?" seemed relevant now.

I thought it was for that period of time but realized now that He meant it for this season we were about to enter. Now, He seemed to bring that question back to me again. Now was the time. Still, there was a tinge of grief attached.

Just before I left for Maryland, I had an email from Joel Rosenberg's Joshua Fund announcing his tour to Israel for the Epicenter Conference in April of 2008. For some reason, I distinctly heard the Lord telling me that I would be going on this trip. As ridiculous as that seemed, I put out a fleece that if I was to go, God would have to provide the funds. I had written out a deposit check, which was due August 1 for the first deposit, but had not sent it in. Judy, my good friend and fellow lover of Israel, told me the tour was already full. Nonetheless, I felt the Lord urge me to do it, so I sent in the deposit with a fleece: "If this is from God, I will get on, even though it is too late and full. If it is not, I'll just get my deposit back. If it is from Him, He will provide the remainder. I cannot discern the will of God in this except by obeying this urge."

In his devotional for August 3, Oswald Chambers wrote, "The great thing to remember is that we go up to Jerusalem to fulfill God's purpose, not our own" (Chambers, Oswald. *My Utmost for His Highest*. Barbour House Publishing. 1963, p. 215.)

CHAPTER THIRTY-FIVE

Back Home Again

(Journal Entry 8/11/07)

*As always, just when I put down on paper my need to spend
more time with John and my need for a sabbatical, the enemy
tries to push in and fill up every second of my time with
busyness.*

After a very busy week catching up on things left undone for a week,
I took John on one of his much-loved trips to Flagstaff, and we had
a lovely day together. Later, finally able to sit down and put my feet up,
thoughts began to wander around in my mind again. Sadness at the
thought of leaving fifteen years of ministry; it was hard imagining my life
without it. And sadness at watching a harvest in the lives of others who
have gone through a long dark night of the soul, while my dark night
continued. But I could no longer sit around mourning these losses; I had
to move in the direction God was leading me.

On that morning, after reading Hannah's cry in 1 Samuel, when
giving back to God the son she had prayed for and then the harvest of
God giving her more children, and God speaking directly to Samuel, I
cried out to God to please speak to me, please give me some tiny thing.
And He did. Amy Carmichael's devotional spoke directly to me from God,
specifically addressing me personally about the pain I felt over the loss of
ministry to women:

You were like a leafy bush, and many little things came for you to shelter. You were not great or important, but you could help those little things.

And it was the joy of your life to help them.

Now you can do nothing at all.

Some desolation—illness, monetary loss, or something you cannot talk about to anyone, a trouble no one seems to understand has overwhelmed you. All your green leaves have gone.

Now you cannot shelter even the least little bird. You are like a bush with its bare twigs. No use to anyone.

That is what you think …

The spring will come again, for after winter there is always spring.

But when will the spring come? When will your bush be green with leaves again? When will the little birds you love come back to you? I do not know. Only I know that Sun and Snow are working together for good. And the day will come when the memory of helplessness and inability to give help to anyone else, or the memory of hard financial times, or of loneliness, loss or isolation—these will all pass as a dream in the night. All that seemed lost will be restored.

Now in the midst of so much unhappiness, engulfing your heart in cold, let these words seep down—like fingers of sunlight, like trickles of first spring rains—to refresh your inmost soul:

He will not fail you, Who is the God of the sun and the snow. (Ibid., p. 109)

Ministering to the women had now been replaced by ministering to John, and this seemed good in His sight. Amen.

CHAPTER THIRTY-SIX

I Know Who Is Taking Me

(Journal Entry 8/21/07)

*It is difficult for me to really know right now what direction
my life is taking. But I know who is taking me. He will not
fail me nor forsake me.*

John had stopped using his CPAP again. He said it kept him awake
at night and irritated his skin. Linda got him a nasal cannula for his
oxygen, so at least he was using that at night.

A loneliness had set in. The never-ending cycle of dementia, not
knowing what was taking place in John's mind or how long it would go
on, gripped me.

Until I went into the sanctuary of my God.

The victory was not in some glorious answer to all of my prayers. The
victory was in the profound discovery that the peace of God does not
depend on outward circumstances. The victory lies in those moments in
our lives when all of the outward circumstances make it seem all hope is
gone, and we discover a peace in our *soul*, a peace that cannot be explained.
It is Him: He is our peace, no matter what is going on around us. Satan
knows nothing of this peace—he rages at it; he fights against it for all he's
worth. But he cannot have it—unless we surrender it to him.

We had planned a camping trip with Linda and Kim, but at the last
minute, the RV wouldn't start and after trying many ways to start it, we
had to let it go. John seemed relieved. He didn't know how to fix it, and
I think he was uncomfortable with going now that I was driving. Later,
during lunch with a friend, Diana Taylor, who is a financial adviser, she

asked how much we paid each month for the RV and how often we used it. Because we had only used it twice that year, she advised we sell it. This brought mixed emotions: relief that we would not have to take long trips with me driving, and great sadness at the ending of a chapter of wonderful trips together. I later read a devotional about Abraham giving up his son in an act of worship. I lay down my much loved-RV as an act of worship.

Bible study was going well, and I sensed a season of anointing coming. Pat called, breathless with excitement of how doors of heaven had seemed to open all week, and God had poured out His anointing on things for which He had given her a vision years ago. Her dark night of the soul—never forgotten—lay just next to a season of anointing as a reminder that none of this is coming from her. Isn't this why He leaves the memory of the dark night—to remain in stark contrast to His working and His harvest? As soon as we forget the utter helplessness of that dark night, the utter unworthiness of anything we ourselves could offer, we quickly move into our flesh, and before long, we are basking in the glory of what is His alone.

He leaves it there so that if we, "look to the right hand—or to the left," we see and are reminded that the dark night was for the dying out of self, so He can live His life through us. We enter into His joy; our joy is fulfilled in His glory.

Dementia triggers the oddest reactions at the oddest times. John and I went to see a movie. There was nothing special about it except it brought up old memories of all the times we had been to the movies, how John used to sing the "Werenberg" song as it played, and I would shush him. Or, how he would pick out someone in the theater and begin a running commentary of his nonsensical dialogue. He always watched all the credits at the end, fascinated about where it might have been filmed, and we sat alone in the theater wondering what exactly a "best boy" did. When we were doing our photography together, I began calling him my "best boy," adding to the already long list of pet names—"My Bear" being my favorite.

At the movies, I always had to ask him silly questions about things I didn't understand, and on this day, sitting beside him, as he looked like the old John in the dark, eating popcorn, I started to lean over and ask him a question about something I didn't understand. Then realized I couldn't ask him. He wouldn't know what I was talking about, and he wouldn't understand my question. Nevertheless, simply out of habit, I did that several times during the movie, and each time, it left me feeling alone and grief-stricken. After the movie, he wanted to watch the credits as I went out to the restroom, and when he came out, he started to tell me that the movie was filmed in New Mexico and started to cry. He could barely speak, his face crumpling into tears. "I think we were there once, but maybe not." And then his standard comment when he couldn't remember something: "It must have been years ago."

A sudden anger choked up into my throat—not anger at John, but at this third entity. An angry war of words thrashed about in my mind: "Of course we were in New Mexico. Why did that make him cry? Who are you! Where is my strong, funny husband—the one who knew everything? What have you done with him?" I hated dementia! I wanted it gone! I wanted to climb back into the passenger seat of the car while he drove again. I wanted everything to be like it used to be.

These thoughts jumbled together in my head in fast and furious succession as we got into the car. I drove, and he gave me his now repetitive weather report in his now monotone voice. At home, he settled back into his chair to watch HGTV, not realizing that he had watched this rerun over and over. I went out to the porch to regain my focus and saw that my beloved Aspen trees seemed to be dying. I was suddenly overwhelmed at this. I loved these trees; I loved to hear them clapping as the wind blew through them. I loved them in winter, their stark white trunks standing out against the blue of the sky. John loved them, too, and we would go on long drives into Flagstaff, looking for the perfect aspen shot, giving us dozens of black-and-white photos.

I sat down and cried, "Please Jesus, don't let the Aspens die."

Just then, John peeked out the door and gave me a weather report.

How long, O Lord?

CHAPTER THIRTY-SEVEN

A Trip to Israel? Really, Lord?

(Journal Entry 9/20/07)

Interesting events appear to be developing for me again. I have not heard anything from the Israel tour and figured I was not going.

Frankly, I was relieved. I would get my deposit back and wouldn't have to worry about getting the rest of the money together. I felt foolish anyway, thinking I could do such an extravagant thing, with John's illness and bills due.

On that Thursday, however, a call came from Inspired Travel, and she happily informed me that I was on for the tour. In my practical thinking, I told her thank you, but I was sorry I would not be able to come up with the money for the October deposit ($500), and I should probably cancel. She said she was sorry, too, and said she would return my deposit.

I felt awful as I had put out a fleece (sending my deposit in past the deadline) and left it up to the Lord to close or open doors. Now He had opened the door, and I had too little faith to take the next step. Here it was again: the issue of trust. My mind flip-flopped, telling me I had done the right thing, while the spiritual side reminded me about obedience and trust. One thing was for certain: I had no peace about my decision.

On Saturday, John and I had planned a trip to Phoenix to see Adam and Jeniece and go to Trader Joe's. It was a very rainy day. A hurricane had hit off the Baja, and remnants of it came up through Wickenberg and Kingman. We were going to Phoenix via Wickenberg, so we headed out through Skull Valley, where we encountered the first of the rain. Low black clouds and pouring rain made for slow driving through Kirkland and Peeple's Valley. However, starting down Yarnell Hill, overlooking the valley below, it was beautiful. The steep, winding drive down Yarnell Hill was not yet drenched in rain, and the expanse of the valley opened up below to a scene John and I loved more than any other—that Arizona scene when the sun peeks through the clouds and shines brilliantly against the backdrop of black clouds, creating a Monetesque impressionistic painting of brilliant light and dark shadows. A distant rainbow completed the picture.

Back home again, the canceled check from the travel agency was in the mail, and my heart felt heavy. On Sunday morning (September 23), the very day that six years ago I had left for Israel, I opened *My Utmost for His Highest*, just as I had that day, and there again was the same verse God had spoken to me then: "Behold, we go up to Jerusalem" (Luke 18:31). I recalled how that had confirmed to me that I was in His will in going to Jerusalem in the midst of such a dangerous time after 9/11. Now it struck a deep, sad chord in my heart. I could see no logical practical reason why I should go, yet I could not escape what the Spirit was speaking to my heart: God wanted me to go on this trip.

On September 25, Linda called to see if she could come over. I was cleaning the kitchen when she got here, and she handed me an envelope. It held a beautiful card telling me of her love for me and a check for $2,000. I started to cry.

She said, "Now you can go to Israel."

I couldn't stop crying. God had planned this all along. Linda had been waiting for an insurance settlement for over a year, and it had just come in. I can't imagine why God wanted me to go to Israel in the middle of all of this, but there it was. Now you can go to Israel. Feeling a little silly after picking up the phone to call the travel agency and putting it down again, I finally made the call. They advised me to return my deposit and registration, and they would see if they could still get me on the tour.

Peace returned.

Later, I opened my Bible to Psalm 102, where I had been reading:

> You will arise and have mercy on Zion; for the time to favor her, yes, the set time has come. For her servants take pleasure in her stones, and show favor to her dust ... This shall be written for the generations to come, that a people yet to be created may praise the Lord. For He looked down from the height of His sanctuary; from heaven the Lord

viewed the earth, to hear the groaning of the prisoner, to release those appointed to death, to declare the name of the Lord in Zion, and His praise in Jerusalem. (Psalm 102: 13–21 NKJV)

CHAPTER THIRTY-EIGHT

A New Neurologist, a New Diagnosis, a New Round of Confusion

(Journal Entry 10-3-07)

After the exam the doctor said he couldn't agree with the diagnosis of frontotemporal/Pick's disease. He does not have Alzheimer's. He doesn't know what is wrong with him, but he definitely has some kind of dementia. Really? What else is new?

In October, I had made an appointment with another neurologist in Sedona. I liked him and so did John. His examination seemed more thorough, and at the end, he declared he didn't think John had frontotemporal dementia or Pick's disease. He said he definitely had some kind of dementia in the frontal lobe but not in the temporal lobes. He wanted us to go to the University of California–San Francisco to see a specialist in the field.

Driving home, confusion spread over us both. Is this what we were supposed to do? We didn't have the kind of insurance that would pay for such a thing, and I had no peace at all about it. John had become so tired and irritated at all of the doctors, and he became agitated and fearful of any change in routine. He definitely did not want to go and told me so. Even if we went to the best dementia expert in the world, could he offer a cure? Could he fix him? I decided to wait on the Lord and see what happened next.

John's friend Darrell, from Alexandria, Virginia, came for a visit the following week, and the two of them went sightseeing around northern

Arizona. I enjoyed the short respites while they were gone. Later, Darrell told me of a strange incident that had taken place while they were in Sedona. John seemed to glaze over and began jabbering and smacking his lips. This alarmed me. Clearly, he had experienced a seizure of some type.

The next day, I was at my computer in the office, while John was sitting in his easy chair. Suddenly, he began laughing, chuckling, and talking jibberish, kidding me about a song. I asked him what he was talking about, but his eyes were glazed and had a sort of wild expression. He was smacking his lips and then his speech became thick, and he was unable to speak. I forced his attention back on me and asked him what day it was and other questions to get him to focus. He thought it was 1997. I called Linda and Kim, and they advised me to get him to the emergency room; he was having seizures.

A year ago, I had done a lot of research on temporal lobe seizures, how they can cause bradycardia and dementia, just as he had been told early on in this disease, but we had not followed up on that at the time. He was now having another kind of seizure, which the ER doctor called "partial complex" seizures. He prescribed an anti-seizure medication, and they sent him home a few hours later.

The questions began swimming around my mind again. What if he had gone with the seizure diagnosis at the beginning and had been on anti-seizure meds all this time? Would he have continued to deteriorate? I just couldn't go back to this place again, however, this confusion, not knowing, wondering if we had made the right decisions, gone to the right doctors, and all of the circular thinking this produced. Of course, the truth is that even if he was having temporal lobe seizures, the research showed that the anti-seizure medications rarely stop the seizures. And, what would cause this kind of seizure activity? It had to be some kind of head trauma, but John hadn't had any head trauma that he knew about. Another mystery to add to the stacks and stacks of mysteries associated with this disease.

During all of this, my friends Diane and Guy had hosted a Mike Wells conference here, and I went to that while Darrell was here with John. The conference added another blessing. I also got a letter in the mail from the travel agency, informing me that I was back on the tour. Well, amen. If God wanted me on this trip, He must know something I didn't.

Dane had a terrible fall on the job and broke his foot. They had no insurance, and the doctors bungled the whole thing terribly. Instead of finding the break, they sent him home from the ER with a sprain diagnosis and a wrapped foot. After much pain and many doctors and X-rays later, it was found he had a badly broken foot, which should have been operated on immediately. Now, more than a month later, it was too late. No one wanted to take him as a patient because he had no insurance, so he had it set in a cast. His business immediately began to suffer, and they were getting further and further behind in bills.

My reaction to all of this—after years of learning to trust God and to believe that He uses everything in life to squeeze us, to draw us back to Himself—resulted in a supernatural calm that God had allowed this and He was in it. Their finances finally got so bad that they were one payment away from not having a place to live. My reading one morning said something about giving to those in need when you have it in your hand to give. I did. So, I gave them $1,000 from the Israel money and knew in my heart that this was part of my training in my new faith lesson, and God would restore it to me double. Never have I felt so certain about anything.

When I first felt I should give them the money, it felt like I was stepping off a cliff with no safety net. After I gave it, however, I found that stepping off a cliff with no safety net but Jesus was the most amazing thing I had ever experienced. All fear left. All of my issues with security and trust vanished. Stepping into the Jordan before God parts the water is vastly different than having Him part the water and then stepping in. This thought I tucked away for future use.

I learned that my dear friend Eunice would be moving away. She had been one of my greatest encouragers during this time. My heart mourned; so many of my close friends had moved since this ordeal began. However, another very close friend, Kim, returned home after her assignment with FEMA ended in New Orleans. How I loved the women God brought into my life—the long lunches and fellowship in the Lord. I was reminded again and again of Malachi 3:16–17: "Then those who feared the LORD spoke to one another, And the LORD listened and heard them; So a book of remembrance was written before Him For those who fear the LORD And who meditate on His name. 'They shall be Mine,' says the LORD of hosts. 'On the day that I make them My jewels. And I will spare them as a man spares his own son who serves him'" (NKJV). We are His jewels, just because we speak to one another about the Lord.

Thanksgiving was really wonderful at Adam and Jeniece's. Our family time around the table was too precious for words. John broke down crying as He thanked God for the men he feeds at the Pioneer Home Care Center in Prescott.

I thank You, even now, Lord Jesus, that You brought ministry into his life even though his mind is leaving. Only You could do something so rare and precious.

CHAPTER THIRTY-NINE

The Dream

(Journal Entry 11/26/08)

John is so much worse. Everyone noticed it at Thanksgiving. I had noticed for so long now that his breathing seemed labored, but when I watched him as he sat watching TV, his chest shows his breathing to be very shallow and difficult.

I had a dream just before Thanksgiving that we were sitting together somewhere, and John expelled a long, murmuring breath and then closed his eyes. I thought he was having a seizure and tried to rouse him, but taking his hand, I felt it was cold, and I knew he had died. The dream was so real—the emotion I felt so real—that I asked God if He was preparing me for what was coming.

Recently, I had been watching John in his sleep, as he lay partly on his back with his elbow bent up in the air and his hand across his forehead. His hand would slip down, and he kept putting it back over his forehead. His breathing was very labored and difficult. I tried to move him onto his side. I later told Linda about this, and she said it was what the medical profession calls "neuro breathing." Patients who have brain disease (usually brain stem tumors) experience this type of breathing. So, this may be part of the disease. I had the sense that my time with him was growing short.

The second week of December, I made a decision that was to become an emotional black hole that I never saw coming. I chose that as the time to sell the RV. We were paying for something we no longer used, and only time would tell whether it was the right decision. It was as though I was closing the door completely on an entire part of my life with John. The anguish was almost unbearable. And I sold it for less than I was asking, making the wound that much deeper. I struggled tremendously as the negotiations continued, fighting back tears that flowed as freely as the winter rain and sleet that had settled over the city. When it came time to clean it out, I called Linda to help me, and together, we hurriedly threw everything into boxes and bags. She moved so fast it didn't give me any time to ruminate over every scrap of memory that was tucked away in that RV, which was her intent of course. I thank God for others who have more discernment than I do in some of these things. I would never have gotten through that part.

The next day I met my friend Kim at Wildflower. My insides felt raw and ripped apart, yet God in His miraculous way poured living water through us both, as we ministered to each other and caught up on two years' worth of lost time. She loaned me a DVD by Louis Giglio called *How Great Is Our God*, which ministered so profoundly to me that I ended up showing it to my Bible study and then to the rest of the family. All of us were brought to tears by the magnificence of our God in His creation.

On December 17, we went to Sun City for John's appointment with the new neurologist, Dr. Marwan Sabbagh, who had been suggested to me three years before by the director of the Alzheimer's Association. Dr. Sabbagh was an expert on dementia. The first thing he did was to interview me in a separate room, which no doctor had ever done. He listened carefully to my observations and wrote down everything as I explained the events of the past several years. I told him my concerns about the seizures and about the breathing and oxygen deprivation, and all the observations I had written over this period of time. He was very pleased to have all of this written down.

Then he interviewed John in a way no other doctor had done. He finally turned to face me and told me he was a plain speaker and would not pull any punches with me. I silently thanked God for that. He explained that John didn't appear to have the classic symptoms of frontotemporal dementia/Pick's disease, although he did have some type of dementia in the frontal lobe. He was more interested in the left temporal seizure activity and the oxygenation levels. He proceeded to schedule several tests, including a portable twenty-four-hour EEG; John would wear an EEG monitor at home.

At the close of the appointment, he took my hands in his and explained that if John had left temporal epilepsy, it could be correctable. "We will get to the bottom of this," he said intently, and I cried.

I was so dazed by this news, by a doctor who cared, that I was speechless. The night before, as I lay in bed next to John, I could feel the whole bed shaking with his every breath, and his body seemed to be twitching. I laid my hands on his back and head as he slept and prayed for his healing like I had never prayed before for anything. After a few hours, I fell asleep.

After the tests were done, we drove home elated. For the first time in three years, a ray of hope had been lifted in my spirits, and I dared to believe that John could get better.

Christmas was a peaceful time at our house with all of the families. God gave me an abundance of energy and strength throughout the holidays.

On Christmas Eve, Dr. Sabbagh had called to tell me that the EEG results showed that John suffered from seizures that started from the time he started to doze off and continued all through the night. He never went into REM sleep. His blood oxygen level was also low. The doctor wanted to change his anti-seizure meds to a new one, and John's first few nights on this new medication were fitful and restless. His breathing seemed worse than usual, and during the day, he slept off and on and was groggy and confused. The side effects of the medicine seemed to mask any improvement, which always seemed to be the case.

CHAPTER FORTY

Hope Dashed

(Journal Entry 12-28-07)

*A friend had given me the DVD "How Great Is Our God"
by Louis Giglio. It rocked my world, transformed my soul.
I showed it to the rest of the family and it seemed to have
the same effect on all of us. Thank You Jesus. These little
interludes in the midst of such sorrow are like little streams
in a dry and weary land.*

Dane and Tasha were undergoing serious financial distress since he
broke his foot. The ortho doctor in Flagstaff confirmed that it was
a very serious break and would need surgery. This caused me such pain.
Seeing my kids suffer under the best of circumstances was painful; seeing
them suffer when I was already so emotionally drained was more than I
wanted to bear. Still, the event seemed to prove Romans 8:28 true: God
worked it together for good and it drew both of them into a deeper walk
with Christ.

John was not doing well at all. He was agitated, had difficulty with
language, slept fitfully, and had lost interest in everything he always loved
doing. We did drive to Phoenix so he could spend some Christian gift
cards, but he was anxious and did not enjoy the trip at all. He seemed very
distraught while in the store and did not want to shop anywhere else. We
drove to his favorite cigar store and then to his favorite restaurant, Mimi's
Café, where he appeared to be anxious and very worried. Gone now, it
seemed, was his ability to enjoy those things that even a few months ago
still made him so happy.

The real test came, however, when we went to our all-time favorite Trader Joe's, and he was reluctant to go inside with me. I was taken captive then to overwhelming sadness, remembering again how John could make a silly trip to Trader Joe's into a grand adventure. John was always like a little kid, wanting to try every new thing—some new and exotic dish to cook. Everything with John was such an adventure. Now, even the Trader Joe's experience turned sour, and driving home, I fought the hot tears stinging my eyes as he sat, stone-faced, beside me.

What happened to the hope of a few short weeks ago? The hope of possible recovery? That hope was dashed, not merely by the realization that if there were improvement it would take some time, but by the fact that he was not only not improving but getting worse. At least on the other medication he was sweet and compliant. Now, he was contrary, argumentative, and more confused than ever.

As I look back, this was a turning point for me as well. My faith was shaky. A carrot was dangled before me—a carrot promising hope. The intense prayers had produced what? John was worse than ever. Doubts closed in from all sides, questions of my own discernment of these things. Was it really God I felt praying through me that night for John, or just me on an emotional high? So many people were watching this thing unfold. I had invited everyone along to participate in the unfolding of God's plan for my life, but once more, it all seemed to be lying in a pile of rubble, and now everyone could watch as I unraveled from disappointment. Lord, do we not see healing here in our Nazareth because we are too far gone in unbelief? Was I wrong to believe that you would heal John?

God had taken me through a very long and detailed process, working into my very fiber what He really means by love, joy, peace, patience, goodness, kindness, faithfulness, meekness, and self-control—all the fruit of the Spirit. He tore down my own emotional love for John and replaced it with His supernatural, unconditional love. He taught me peace in the midst of agonizing emotional pain. He seemed to now be uncovering His own version of hope—hope that does not disappoint (Romans 5:5). What is hope? Hope is the fulfillment of His promises written in His Word. Was He asking me to hope when all possibility of an answer was gone?

I didn't manufacture this hope of John getting better. The doctor held it out to me, like a golden egg on a silver platter. I had felt hope in Maryland last July, when John was showing signs of life and I began to pray for his healing.

I do not even pretend that I was not now involved in an intense struggle with my faith. Watching the Times Square New Year's Eve celebrations on TV, all I could think was, *Why are they all so happy? What in this dark world is there to be happy about?* My friend Mary's son, who we had prayed over for so many years with an ongoing illness, died a few days after Christmas. I had such difficulty at the memorial service, sitting in the back row so I could make a fast exit, tears flowing freely.

Fear hit me that day. Fear that one day I would be sitting in the front pew of that same church sanctuary at my husband's funeral. Fear that what if I lost one of my own sons? Dane's fall got too close for comfort. There was also fear that through this process, my own faith would fail. It felt like it was failing now. God identified my fears quickly, however, and cleared them out immediately.

Jesus prayed that Peter's faith would not fail as he was being sifted by the enemy. His prayer was answered. He was praying that same prayer for me now. I was assured that my faith would not fail, because Jesus Himself was praying for me.

On January 15, 2008, Dr. Sabbagh's office called that they had a cancellation and wanted to know if we could come in that day. After hearing about John's side effects, the doctor changed his meds. I told him about the things I had observed, and he determined the meds weren't helping the seizures at all. Hopefully, the new one he ordered would help. He was still not convinced John had a classic dementia, but he wouldn't know until he got the seizures under control.

He told me he thought John probably never needed the pacemaker, which I always suspected. He also explained that he was just putting out fires right now; once he got the seizures under control, he would deal with the next fire. I asked if the seizures were the whole problem and could the lost memory be restored. He said possibly, but he couldn't promise that, explaining that memory is in the temporal lobes and personality is in the frontal lobe. The brain is an amazing and complicated organ. Does anyone really know what goes on there, or is it all just guessing games?

John was unusually lucid while there, forming complete sentences and smiling a lot. The doctor said if he had Pick's disease, he wouldn't be able to do that at all. So, Pick's was ruled out.

The first morning on the new meds, taken together with the Keppra, the new anti-seizure medication, made John extremely confused and unable to even speak well. He was confused over the identity of my niece, who was visiting for the day, which was unusual for him. Visiting with

Nat, Linda, and good friend Chris later revived my spirits. My whole life seemed tied up now with going to the doctor, picking up prescriptions, and keeping John comfortable and calm. so every little change in that routine was vital to my well-being. There was no laughter in my home any longer. Laughing with these ladies was sweet water to my parched soul.

The doctor scheduled John for a sleep study, and I took advantage of the time alone to draw near to God, singing and praying. While he was away, I was aware that the very air—the atmosphere—in my house cleared. If I could describe the difference, I would, but it was as though the actual air around me was crystal clear and I could think and pray again. I was hearing from God—I felt Him! I had lived in such a cloud of dementia that I had forgotten what it felt like to be out from under it.

When John came home the next morning, he was worse than ever. He slept most of the day, and when awake, his speech was thick and slurred. I, too, slept off and on all day, treating myself to a true Shabbat rest.

CHAPTER FORTY-ONE

From Shabbat Rest to New Crisis

(Journal Entry 1/25/08)

I cannot believe the manner in which events in my life can change so dramatically in one week. One week ago, I was resting in a Shabbat as John had seemingly gone from bad to worse; the next day (1/19/08) his ongoing complaints of pain in his upper left abdomen became acute and I took him to the ER.

The ER doctor performed a series of tests and finally determined John had pancreatitis and admitted him. His pain level and the blood work showed elevated levels of the enzymes associated with the pancreas; however, he had none of the classic symptoms of pancreatitis. Again, something was terribly wrong, but no one was certain what it was. He was scheduled for an abdominal CT, and the doctor explained that he wanted to rule out pancreatic cancer. John had been complaining about this pain in his abdomen for at least six to eight months, but I had not been able to get anyone to follow up with it. Now it seemed that it may have been chronic pancreatitis, which could have damaged the pancreas.

After he was admitted, another doctor examined him and scoffed at the diagnosis of pancreatitis. This doctor was arrogant and curt. I was faced once again with the tedious task of explaining to all of the medical personnel that John had dementia; that he couldn't understand what they were asking; that he didn't know what they meant when they asked him to describe his pain on a scale of one to ten. All the while, he ignored their questions and tried to tell them of some polyps that were removed a few years ago.

Advocating for John was exhausting, and for the following three days, I repeated this same scenario again and again. I thought, *Why doesn't someone ask me where my emotions were on a scale of one to ten!*

Another gastroenterologist specialist was called in who explained that due to the inflammation of the pancreas and the weight loss (John had been losing weight consistently over the past several months), they needed to rule out cancer and would follow up in a couple of weeks with another CT.

This talk of the dreaded C word, added to the dreaded D word, sent my emotions on a wild tangent. Hope given by the neurologist that he could possibly get better turned into hope ripped away as he only got worse. Now a new, unexplainable health issue, more doctors scratching their heads, and possibly cancer of a sort that could take him in months.

I had a meltdown that Sunday night. Alone in the house, trying to sleep, I suddenly shouted into the dark, my voice sounding alarmingly loud even to me, "Where are You in all of this! How can any of this bring glory to You? I cry and cry out to You, and there is no answer, only confusion piled on top of confusion. I rejoiced to think of his healing, and now I resign myself to his death, but You withhold any information from me. I am not allowed to grieve; I am not allowed to hope. What do You want?"

I did not go back to my usual, "Nevertheless, I will trust You," before I finally drifted off to sleep in the wee hours.

Paul Beard was to be here that Tuesday. My house was a disaster. I hadn't shopped for food. Even though John was very sick, they discharged him later that afternoon. In all of this roiling, dark cloud cover in my home, I was amazed to find that a simple trip to Wal-Mart by myself felt like a vacation.

It always surprised me how I could go to bed so exhausted, scared, and hopeless, yet wake up with a strange renewal of hope. Weeping does indeed endure for a night, but joy comes in the morning, and that is the miracle of this walk of faith in the dark. God was not at all bothered or threatened or even angry by my fits of despair and the pounding of my fists against His chest. He knew. He knew my walking through this wilderness.

I got an e-mail from my friend Kim, telling me that since she was not on assignment, she had a lot of time and energy on her hands. She wanted to know if she could come and do some housecleaning for me. This was a need I had not shared with anyone. She heard it directly from God, and now I had my house cleaned.

There was something so much bigger going on here than I could get my mind around. I was being "battered into use" as Oswald Chambers writes.

The anchor holds

Paul's visit was good for me. He made me laugh again. He is so like John once was. Now, however, John only sat stone-faced, unable to banter with Paul as he used to do, with me as the object of their entertainment. They used to come up with endless ways to get to me, and it always worked. I always fell into uncontrollable laughter, even when their humor was aimed at me! It was always affectionate humor. We had an impromptu jam session, with Paul playing his latest resonator guitar and my niece's husband, Paul, singing with his acoustic. We laughed a lot that evening. The irony did not escape me, however. Two nights ago, my lone cry of anguish went up to God in the silence, and now, this night, the house was filled with children, music, and laughter.

What a life this was.

CHAPTER FORTY-TWO

And on Another Note ...

(Journal Entry 1/25/08)

And on another note, the Israel trip—still up in the air with all of the goings on of the past several weeks—looms ahead. The deadline for the final deposit is today and I still have no idea what God would have me do. John could be completely well by then, or in the last throes of death.

I waited this day for some word. That morning I read Mark 15:41: "and many other women who came up with Him to Jerusalem ..."

Not much to go on. I fasted for the day. The sleep clinic called and reported that John's sleep study showed that he had seventy-one sleep apneas per hour. How could it be that he breathes at all? That means he stops breathing over once a minute. This doctor felt certain that if the sleep apnea was under control, it would control the seizures and the dementia.

Really?

Before all of this began, John had none of these problems. He slept soundly and woke up full of energy and ready to go every morning. How could seizures just start for no reason; or sleep apnea for that matter? All of this had a sudden beginning back in the fall of 2004. Mystery upon mystery upon mystery. Would I ever have a clear diagnosis?

I had asked my friends Eunice and Kim to pray with me about the Israel trip. Calling the travel agency to see what would happen if I had to cancel my trip due to John's illness, or even his death, I discovered that I would have to pay the full amount and even possibly penalties. It seemed, then, that it was out of my hands. Checking my savings account, which I had been putting funds into from time to time for the trip, I had all but $800 for the remainder of the deposits. My mom offered to help cover that last expense, so now the trip was paid for, and it looked like I was going to Israel. I still couldn't fathom God's plan in all of this, but it certainly seemed He wanted me to go.

On January 29, Kim came to clean my house. What a blessing. I left with John to pick up the sleep apnea report, do some shopping, and have lunch. John's usual excitement at shopping was completely gone now. He had no interest in those things. The sleep apnea report showed he had several events of something called Cheynes-Stokes breathing pattern, which was the breathing pattern I had noticed. Looking on the Internet, I saw that possible causes for this were related to heart failure, kidney failure, lack of oxygen to body tissues, apoxia, or stroke. Combined with neck pain (which he now complained of constantly), it could also be related to encephalitis. Based on what I knew, He had none of those things, with the exception of lack of oxygen.

CHAPTER FORTY-THREE

But You, Be Strong in the Lord

(Journal Entry 2/5/08)

But you, be strong and do not let your hands be weak, for your work shall be rewarded. (2 Chronicles 15:7 NKJV)

One thing I have desired of the LORD, that I will seek: That I may dwell in the house of the LORD all the days of my life, to behold the beauty of the LORD; and to inquire in His temple. For in the time of trouble He shall hide me in His pavilion; in the secret place of His Tabernacle He shall hide me; He shall set me high upon a rock ... Therefore I will offer sacrifices of joy in His tabernacle; I will sing, yes, I will sing praises to the Lord (Psalm 27:4–6 NKJV)

Do not be afraid. From now on you will catch men. (Luke 5:10 NKJV)

On Tuesday, John, still very sick, still in a great deal of pain, was sitting on the couch and motioned for me to come over. I sat down next to him. He was reading A. W. Tozer's *The Pursuit of God* and wanted to share a passage with me. He began reading in his weak and shaky voice from Matthew 11:28, "Come unto Me ..." Then he read, childlike, as though he had to sound out every word, Tozer's commentary on the verse, ending with his prayer, which began "Lord, make me childlike." The tears ran down my face like rivers as I watched him, with a sweet and tender sincerity, praying this prayer from his heart. It was the most tender, most

161

precious moment perhaps in all of our lives together. Then he went to lie down, and I told the Lord, "If those are the last words he were to ever speak to me, I will have known that You had accomplished everything in him that You intended." And I yielded him up to Jesus once more.

On Valentine's Day, I took John to get a haircut and then he wanted to buy a Valentine's card for me. My heart was wrenched by these acts of sweet kindness. He had never missed a Valentine's Day in all of our years together, and even now, almost too weak to walk, he still wanted to find just the right card. I didn't know how much more my heart could stand of this. Please God, please! Give me an answer. Is he dying? Does he have cancer? Is this the end, and if so, why can I not at least know it, so my heart can finally give way to grief that has closure?

Later, after he had gone to bed, I sat up for a long time. The oppression of this disease hung in the air—tangible, thick, sticky, and dark. Death felt as though it were crouching here, lurking around every corner, taunting, vaunting itself the way it did with my mother-in-law, Janet, and then with Dad. It was as though this dark thing, whatever it was, was controlling the final outcome and had the right to torment me with this control.

After getting into bed, watching John with his hand raised, holding onto his forehead, I cried out to God once more, "This is torture! It is torture to watch!" And then it struck me: this torture was not from God—it was from the enemy, who, in his usual deceptive way, was trying to make me believe that he was in control and could use death to control and frighten me. So, I sat up and began to declare that this was a lie. Jesus Christ conquered death; conquered the sting of death. He alone controlled the circumstances and the timing of John's death, and in the name of Jesus Christ and the power of His shed blood and resurrection, I ordered the powers of darkness out of this house, out of John's weakened physical and mental state. Vultures, hyenas that seemed to be hovering over the weak creature, waiting to devour, be gone! Depart from me all you workers of iniquity!

I went into my prayer room and read Romans 8: 26–39 aloud and with authority. Then I slept on the couch, not able to listen to the gasping for air and bizarre seizure sounds. With my iPod playing gentle praises in my ears, I slept one more night.

The anchor holds.

The following morning, a passage of Scripture from 2 Samuel 21:10–14 came to mind about a woman, Rizpah, whose husband had been killed in battle and left to die in the open field. She lay next to him and shooed the vultures until he could be buried. Abraham, waiting for God to appear and walk between the cut pieces of the covenant, spent the night chasing away the birds of prey from the sacrifice.

Max Lucado's precious gem of a book, *Safe in the Shepherd's Arms: Hope and Encouragement from Psalm 23*, spoke tenderly to my bleeding heart from Psalm 23 of walking through the valley of the shadow of death: "The Good Shepherd knows the path. There are dark and narrow valleys. The path is dangerous, poisonous plants can infect the flock. Wild animals can attack the flock. There are narrow trails and dark valleys. He will lead them to the mountain" (Lucado, Max. *Safe in the Arms of the Shepherd: Hope and Encouragement from Psalm 23*. Nashville, TN: Thomas Nelson, Inc., 2002, p. 56).

My heart cries out to You, O Lord. I close my eyes here, and I see a long, dark hallway with no light at all, only You asking me, urging me, to trust You! This is the hardest thing You have ever asked me to do, and You seem to have put this light at the end—a trip to Israel, which seems completely impossible at this time. I am so afraid. I am so afraid. Nevertheless, I have no choice but to trust You. In this hallway, there are no doors to escape through. There are no choices—do I stay or do I escape? No, there is no escape. If John is walking through the valley of the shadow of death, let the shadow be the shadow of Your wings, not the shadow of the wings of the vultures.

CHAPTER FORTY-FOUR

You Have Known My Soul in Adversity

(Journal Entry 2/9/08)

But I trust in the Lord. I will be glad and rejoice in Your mercy, for You have considered my trouble; You have known my soul in adversity and have not shut me up into the hand of the enemy; You have set my feet in a wide place. (Psalm 31:6b–8 NKJV)

John had the second CT on his abdomen, and afterward, I took him to breakfast. His appointment with the gastro doc was scheduled for that Wednesday. For the past four weeks, I had watched him go downhill so fast. My heart was prepared to hear the worst, but in the back of my mind, I fear. Fear what? Fear that I will hear the dreaded word "cancer" and my pain will be inconsolable? Or another fear, fear that I will hear the dreaded words, "Everything is normal," while he seemed near to death, and I would have yet one more mystery disease with which to deal. How could he be so sick if everything was normal?

The doctor's office called a few days after the CT and joyfully announced, "Everything is normal!" John got into his head that the dye contrast they gave him before the test had healed him and then he immediately began to get better. I felt like a cruel joke had been played on me again. All the enemies of my soul had been taunting, torturing, hovering, threatening, and gathering. Now, they were laughing, mocking me. I had e-mailed someone in our Sunday school class to see if the pastor and deacons could come and pray over him. Later, one of them called to tell me that our beloved Pastor Chris had been walking out of the building, on his way to pray for John, when he fell and broke his foot. As they were closing the door to the ambulance, he called out for someone to go pray for John, so another friend of John's, Joe Thompson, came over that afternoon to pray for him. I cannot describe the enormous peace and relief I felt after he left. Having someone else here, someone else praying and talking to John, seemed to take a heavy load off my shoulders.

Reading the precious card he bought me for Valentine's Day brought bittersweet tears. I bought him a coffee-table book of beautiful photo scenes of America, which he pored over for the next several months. He had taken to these types of books, so I bought them whenever I found one. He would sit on the porch and look at them again and again as he dozed off and on. That night we went to Sweet Tarts, a favorite restaurant, which he enjoyed. He was definitely feeling better—Joe's prayers?

Adam called and he, too, wanted to come up and say a prayer over John. Later, Dane came and then Paul and Heather. I can't describe the joy in my heart at having a house full of family again. I had been family-starved.

The next Sunday, John and I went to Sunday school for the first time in four weeks, and it was so good to get back. Our teacher taught on the subject of demonic activity, and after class, I asked if he would come over and pray through my house and outside. He agreed. The deacon who was going to come and pray with the pastor had also been taken with a sudden illness—another medical mystery—and I didn't think any of those things were coincidences. After church, Adam prayed a powerful prayer and anointed John. Afterward, the house again felt peaceful and light. John wanted to read to Adam from Tozer's book, a sweet blessing to us all. Everyone else came later, and again, our house was filled with laughter and family.

Writing about it later, I was struck with the thought that in a roundabout way, many of my prayers of all those years were being answered. John, in this new place of dementia, enjoyed my sons and grandchildren, calling them "our sons" instead of "Kathy's sons." Four years ago, he couldn't tolerate having everyone here. Four years ago, Dane had been walking away from the Lord. Now, after the broken foot and financial trials, he and Tasha were walking with the Lord once more. My prayers for John to not be so proud, so raunchy, so uncaring for others, had all been answered. He would be insulted now to be told that he used to be quite crude in his speech. And my prayers that John would fall in love with Jesus Christ had also most definitely been answered. The things God had done in me through this process are absolutely indescribable. So, was God working it all together for good and for His glory? He was.

I had finally managed to get John's CPAP machine working. Since he hadn't used it for awhile it was necessary for it to be recalibrated, and he started using it again. The first few nights he slept badly, but then he began to sleep better, having less seizures I think, but it was difficult to tell. After another few days, he was noticeably better. Sitting on the couch one afternoon, he blurted out, "I've been missing you." He said he felt better, wasn't so sleepy. Then he turned around as I sat working on my computer and said, "I love you." It felt like my old John was back. Later, talking on the phone to a cousin, he described to her perfectly what had been going on with him since 2004. He seemed more focused, clearheaded.

I will ponder these things in my heart, Lord, until You verify for me what is going on.

Kathleen Beard

CHAPTER FORTY-FIVE

I Am Never Going to Recover!

(Journal Entry 2/25/08)

Again, I must not trust in the ups and downs and the ins and outs of dementia.

After a few days, he was again dozing in his chair all day, and when he dozed, his breathing caused his shoulders to rise and fall sharply. His chest barely moved, as though breath was coming only from his throat and not his lungs. One particular day he was very confused. He referred to our granddaughter Ardara as "Ara," not remembering her name.

As we sat on the couch and looked at old photo albums together, which he so enjoyed, he would spontaneously grab my hand, as though memories would surface and cause him to reach for me.

In the long hours of the night, my mind traced across all of the events of my life: *Why am I going to Israel? Is it just me, persuading myself that God wanted me to go? Who in their right might would leave a sick husband and go overseas to a country where war is a constant threat?* I couldn't really bear to think of leaving John. *Would he really be okay while I was gone? What if my being gone threw him into a worse place, and when I returned, what little emotional contact we do have would be lost forever?*

I had bought a book written by caretakers of family members with dementia, and it wrenched my heart to see all of my own emotional roller-coaster rides in there. I was not alone in these crazy feelings after all. I read of spouses secretly wishing their loved one would die and then clutching to hope they would recover. Then, that hope was snatched away. I saw that future, forlorn fear, wondering if life would ever be different or if I would ever recover. That was the worse fear for me, picking away in the back of my mind: *I am never going to recover from this.*

However, as always, I awoke the following morning with peace. I couldn't imagine why, after such emotional turmoil of the long nights, I was still able to wake up with this amazing peace. But, I was not going to question that; it was the one stable constant.

One Sunday, our pastor had preached on the lessons he learned from God as he began the long recovery process from his badly broken foot. He related how, as he lay in the ER, God had led him to pray for others there. Then, almost as if God spoke out loud to me, He reminded me of what He had instructed me three years ago from Acts 16. Pastor Chris said, "And what did Paul and Silas do in the prison cell? They sang and they prayed!" Imagine that: another reminder from God of His word to me from two years ago.

In Sunday school, our teacher continued with the thought, as he used the life of David—his dramatic ups and downs, the hope given, the promises made and then snatched away. David always allows us to see his inner turmoil—his faltering faith. Yet, in the end, he returns to praise for the God he loved and trusted no matter what.

During church and Sunday school, God seemed to be giving me insight for the upcoming trip, and I began jotting it down. The plan was to have some of the men in the Sunday school class visit John, bringing him meals, and as I began writing down names of the men in the class who John knew well and felt comfortable with, it was exactly the number I would need to cover for the time I would be gone. God showed me from His perspective how this would bless these men as well as be a blessing to John. He also showed me that it would be preparation for the time I would need to call some of them to allow me to leave when John needed more full-time care.

I finally had peace about going. God would take care of John, just as He had taken care of us all along.

Later, as he so often does, the enemy attempted to resurrect once more the questioning of my decisions over the past three years, all the old self-blame that he loved to hold over me. This time, instead of going down that dead-end road, I turned to face Jesus Christ, asking Him to judge these emotions before they went off on a tangent. I felt His presence strongly in the room, as though He were giving me a little shake and speaking audibly to my spirit. "All of this has been filtered through Me. If I had not allowed these events in John's life, he would never have been set free from the bondage that has held him captive all of his life. He would have continued in his self-sufficiency and his pride. This hasn't been just for you. Kathy, it has been for him, too."

I was suddenly bowed down with humility and awe. Yes, my Lord. I submit to You in all that You are doing.

The things I began learning from a new book, *The Rest of the Gospel* by Dan Stone (Stone, Dan. *The Rest of the Gospel*. Corvalis, OR: One Press, 2000), given to me by a friend, were like chain cutters—breaking off of me things that still came to me in the nights. Stone compares the trials of our faith to a hurricane. In our soul, where all of the turmoil takes place, there are waves of conflicting emotions, but in our spirit—the eye of the hurricane—where the real Power (Jesus Christ) is, there is calm and peace.

At this new insight, the powerful words God spoke to me on that night jerked me away from the waves and turmoil, and for those blessed few moments, all of time seemed suspended as I heard Him speak. I saw the reason for all of this. I saw that it had a beginning, and it will have an end. I saw that I would recover. Whether the end involved John's healing or going home, God had a reason for all of it.

CHAPTER FORTY-SIX

The Disease Is in the Brain Stem

(Journal Entry 3/4/08)

The sudden twists and turns, extreme changes, sharp and rapid drops from mid-air, continue on their relentless attempts to seduce me into total insanity.

John had a study done to determine if a new development—difficulty swallowing—was due to the dementia or something else. The speech therapist who did the study came out afterward and explained very carefully, and in terms I understood, that John's tongue had become very weak at the base, preventing food and liquid to be pushed down in a normal fashion. He felt John was aspirating fairly consistently. This, he explained, was caused by a neurological problem such as dementia, Parkinson's, or a stroke. Since the part of the brain that controls these involuntary mechanisms is the brain stem, perhaps the dementia was now involved in the brain stem, which usually happened in late-stage dementia. He said they could do some speech therapy to try to strengthen his tongue, but I asked him if John was moving into the last stages, how much should I do to treat all the things that would now come up? Was he going to be made more comfortable by doing this, or more anxious? John had such difficulty understanding and following instructions. To take him in several times a week would really add to his anxiety.

The doctor understood what I was asking and said that I should get together all of John's medical records and sit down with his doctor to discuss future options and plans. He said that the speech therapy would not cure the problem, since it is a brain stem problem, and John would eventually need to have a feeding tube.

I called my niece Kim to talk about this, and she was surprised that John was already at that stage. I was surprised as well. In so many ways, he seemed to be holding steady with the progress of the disease, but now there was evidence that he truly was in the latter stages. Once again, back to preparing for his death. Getting all the paperwork started for long-term care now seemed inevitable. God seemed to be saying "Now" to making plans and taking the next steps. My mind would not compute this new information. The outer bands, what they call the "dirty" side of the hurricane, seemed to be roiling toward me once more.

And then, suddenly, overnight, instead of spending all his days dozing in the chair, John again seemed to be full of a manic, restless energy. He was nervous and pacing, but quite cheerful, unable to sit still, talking nonstop. He claimed he was better—his memory was returning, he wanted to begin going to the Pioneer Home to feed the aging men every day instead of twice a week, and he reminded me constantly that we had talked about going to Phoenix the following Monday. His enthusiasm was high and he was smiling, telling me he loved me and hugging me often.

He also wanted to take control again, demanding things, dictating his agenda for each day. If he wanted to go somewhere (at the moment it was a drive to Phoenix) and I told him I was tired, he would reply, "Oh, OK. Well, we will go. It's OK, we can go."

Pat's family was coming up that weekend. My nephew Gene's Russian wife, Olga, was excited to have her parents from Russia visiting, and they were all to be here for a couple of days. I had been very tired from allergies, and John had been pressuring me to take him to Phoenix. But I needed some downtime, a respite. I didn't want to be irritable with John, and sometimes it seemed that irritability spilled out before I even knew it was there. I realized how quickly things could escalate. As long as everything was going smoothly, no major distractions, I was fine. When there were weeks where I had too much to do, too many people to talk to, or anything that took my mind off the problems at hand, I fell into the trap of thinking I couldn't handle any of it. I knew I was not alone in this: all caretakers experience it. It is a sign that they need a respite, and I was very much aware that I needed one now.

Sunday was our typical noisy family gathering, but I really enjoyed it. John seemed to be enjoying himself, although he got tired when he was not able to sit comfortably. I could see that he was tired, but he didn't want to leave. He loved being with people now, and the more the merrier, unlike the days when he was always hurrying me out of these gatherings.

Pat had told me earlier that Gene had written a song about me, so I asked him about it. As others heard us talking, they urged him to sing it to me. Although he didn't feel he had polished it enough, he agreed. We all went into the living room, and I sat next to him. As he began singing in the soft and tender voice I loved, I felt as though he had reached deep down into my heart and overheard my private thoughts. I was stunned. How could he have known?

You're stronger than you know.
You're fire burning white
You look to see how much you've grown
But oh, oh
When the rain becomes a flood
And you fall into a rut
Walk these lonely streets
In this emptiness
You're not alone.
Back to the wall
Hope is nurtured, standing tall
You weather the storm as a guiding light
In courage you soar

Mourning the loss, can't let it go
Can't get off, just along for the ride
And there he is, standing by your side

Turn on the light, catch the air you breathe
Breathe the air he gives, feeling incomplete
Dry your eyes, sit up straight, take your pen and sail to the other side
Your destination on the winds of inspiration
You minister
You're not alone
You minister.
(Joseph Eugene Lutz, 2008)

I wept and wept. This, coming from my dear nephew who had written long correspondence—such sweet letters—while he served as a missionary in Russia. And when his life in that desolate and dark place became more disappointing and his faith was crashing, we traded long, difficult e-mails—he thrashing and wrestling, me trying to hold him up, keep him from drowning—until he finally came home feeling defeat. It seemed the long winter of his soul had finally passed.

Gene told me that he had this song in his heart for over a year. The tune was there, but suddenly the words came like a flood. It was an anointing. It was from God.

I was speechless. But there was something so much bigger there. If my suffering had been seen by others—if others saw something in this that I myself was not able to see, how could I murmur against the pain? This "knowing God"—leading to the "power of His resurrection" and all tied up in the "fellowship of His suffering," a mystery that none of us will ever comprehend this side of eternity—left me without words. Words have not been written to describe how deeply this moved me. As I travel on, not strong! Not full of mountain-moving faith, not casting sycamore trees into the midst of the sea, but crying, grieving, questioning, doubting, fearing, and yes, screaming mad. Yet, if God still manifested Himself in it, there was something much bigger going on in this thing He calls the "fellowship of His sufferings." And I dare not even gaze at it. It is a holy thing.

Monday, I consented to drive John to Phoenix. What once would have been a crazy trip to all of our favorite stores and restaurants was now a painful reminder of the loss of John. He had the radio turned to his favorite jazz station while I had on my iPod to listen to praise and worship. As Michael W. Smith and then Third Day began the strains of Agnus Dei—"Holy, holy, holy are You Lord God Almighty. Worthy is the Lord, worthy is the Lord. You are holy"—my mind finally got untwisted from the web of dementia and I saw Him. I saw Jesus. I would go to Phoenix for Him today. I would serve Jesus. I loved John out of Jesus, not out of myself.

And it turned into a perfectly lovely day. John so enjoyed driving by the house where he grew up and then eating at a Greek restaurant, though he no longer appreciated the exotic foods and ordered a hamburger!

The following day, I went to Pat's retreat (her house) in Dewey to spend the day working on taxes and other paperwork that I was not able to do while John was around. While there, I called to some of the caretaker services offered; it seemed time to take advantage of some of these now. I was so grateful to have this house to run to when things got to be too much at home. God provided many little blessings like this.

CHAPTER FORTY-SEVEN

And I Am Going to Israel?

(Journal Entry 3/31/08)

The last month has been spent in activity in preparation for the Israel trip. Jesus ministered to me day by day—instructing me as to what to do each day to prevent me from feeling overwhelmed by it all.

John's health had improved significantly, and he was so sweet all month, unfazed about my going. I had made all the plans. I would take him to his doctor appointment on March 31 in Phoenix, and he would spend the first week there with Adam. Adam would bring him back to Prescott the following Sunday and make sure he got settled in. Mom would be here to check on him, as well as Linda and Dane, so it felt safe for me to leave him. His chief concern was his meals, and God took care of all of that with several couples from our Sunday school class who offered to bring him meals and visit with him. He was genuinely looking forward to this it seemed.

Still, I went through a period of mourning and sadness over the thought of leaving him. Sometime during the month, he had decided to get rid of most of his favorite shirts and many jackets and pants as if he were preparing for something. Jesus allowed me to grieve—to question—but in the end, He reminded me of my time with Him when Dad was dying, when He asked me, "Am I enough?" So again, I answered, seven years later, "Yes, Lord, You are enough."

I had asked Jesus to do with me now what He did then: remove my human, emotional attachment to my husband and to begin only a supernatural attachment that would not keep me on this roller coaster. He seemed to be doing just that.

And now, one day away from Israel, I finally allowed the excitement to settle over me. I was in a completely amazing place of peace, just as I was before I went in 2001. I was thrilled to be privileged to attend a world prophecy conference with so many prominent Israeli leaders and world-renowned speakers, all addressing the most important world events perhaps in all of history. All of this would take place on the sixtieth anniversary of Israel (or as one speaker, said the 2,560th anniversary).

All of this would have been enough, but Jesus added to it, as He did on 2001: my dear husband's own approval. Several days before I was to leave, he came to me and tenderly handed me a verse he had copied out of A. B. Simpson's book on the Holy Spirit. In his weak and precious voice, John said God had given him this to send with me. The verse said, "Tarry ye in Jerusalem until ye are endued with power from the Holy Spirit" (Luke 24:48 KJV).

On the day I was to leave, my reading was in the Psalms, and appropriately, it was my life verse, Psalm 63:1-8. Judy and Darrell, who were also going on the trip, had wanted to pay for my plane fare and hotel room to LA and back, which then left me with money to spend in Israel.

You are enough, Lord Jesus. You are more than enough. You have given me abundantly above and beyond all that I could hope or imagine.

The day before leaving for Israel, John had a doctor's appointment with Dr. Sabbagh. I explained to the doctor about John's breathing and swallowing difficulty. As I spoke, he put his pen down and sighed, "Oh no." He explained that the disease was in the brain stem, that we were looking at feeding tubes and ventilators in the near future. I heard in the back of my mind, *John is dying.* The doctor couldn't give me a time frame; it could be a year or months, depending on how fast the progression continued. If he stabilized at this stage, it could go on longer.

Leaving him at Adam's, I felt such deep, deep sorrow, yet also a sort of closure. We had something definite instead of yet one more, "everything is normal." This was not normal. All my suspicions about the strange breathing pattern were confirmed, and it all made sense to me. So then, why, when the doctors listened to his lungs, did they sound normal? And why, when they did a CT of his lungs, were they clear? His breathing problem was not from a lung problem; it was a brain problem, and that was what would take him in the end.

Looking back, it seemed so odd that in the midst of all of this, God would have almost forced me to go to Israel. I couldn't explain it. I still can't explain it. While in Israel—the most amazing fourteen days of my life perhaps—I spoke with John Moser, the executive director of Joshua Fund and told him of my love for Israel and my desire to serve with the Joshua Fund in the future. He and his wife and I had a good conversation about this, and I felt we made a real connection. All the while I was there, I sensed strongly in my spirit that God was giving me an outline for His future plans for me. I tucked it all away, not daring to think that far ahead. After returning home, I wrote an essay about my trip and of all the insights He had given me to share with folks back home. Israel is the key to all prophecy, and no one better defines the strategic importance of these events than Joel Rosenberg, author of many books on events in the Middle East and prophecy. So, while John would soon cross the threshold into that eternal home, I was to be left here to complete the ministry God had begun in me so many years before. I can only marvel now at what all of this would mean later.

CHAPTER FORTY-EIGHT

My Only Assignment Is John

(Journal Entry 4/20/08)

*Home from Israel. My assignment is John. I was exhausted
from the trip, from jet lag, and from a head cold I had caught
at the end of the trip, in the Garden Tomb.*

The head cold lasted for the remainder of April and then kicked into
allergies, causing me to be so terribly fatigued during the entire month
of May that I thought I was not going to get through all of the May
activities. It felt like the old Epstein-Barr I had in the late 1980s.

John did very well while I was gone. He so enjoyed all of the visitors
and food, he couldn't wait to tell me all about it. He loved my Israel
pictures and suddenly had a deep and profound love for the Jewish people.
Another of my prayers was answered, that John would share my love for the
Land of Israel. My Sunday school class and then the church wanted me to
do a talk on my trip. This kept me busy, trying to get all of the photos ready
for my niece Kim to put together one of her fabulous DVDs with music.

Adam graduated from college on May 3, which brought a joy to my
heart that surprised me. It felt like so many years of his own feelings
of rejection all melted away as he walked down that aisle to receive his
diploma. Pete came from Florida, and I think it meant more to Adam
than anything else that Pete was proud of him. His grandmother, Ruth
Chinnock, who always wanted to see her children and grandchildren finish
their formal educations, was also unabashedly proud of him, which meant
a lot to him and to me.

The May procession of birthdays, Mother's Day, and get-togethers continued unabated, and I was feeling so much stress and pressure on top of John's obvious decline. I had no time to get the yard ready for summer. Allergies, fatigue, and an unrelenting wind all combined to create a rather unpleasant month.

The government issued stimulus checks to boost the economy, so I scheduled a contractor to build a pergola on our front porch to keep the heat off the front of the house during the summer. This occupied much of my spare time. It turned out wonderfully, and I was so glad I went ahead and did that. I also hired someone to clean our yard, which took a load off my mind. I spoke to the Sunday night church service of my Israel trip, and all in all, we managed to survive another very busy May. John now seemed to enjoy the hustle bustle of our lives; he went everywhere with me, dozing off but happy to be there.

June didn't slow down either. Dane continued to experience pain in his foot, yet the Lord was doing a painstaking and precious inner work in his spirit. Clearly, this had been in His plan all along to draw Dane back—not as he was before, but completely changed. And then Jesus sent a bona fide miracle. A couple from Dane and Tasha's church, good friends, felt led by God to give the tithe from their recent house sale to Dane to have his foot surgery! So, on June 4, he had the surgery and now could begin to heal. What a relief for us all.

John was not doing well now, however. He had done well while I was gone, but during May and June, his breathing seemed worse than ever. He was terribly weak, no longer able to walk around much. He still wanted to go everywhere I went but would find the nearest chair and sit down while I did my grocery shopping. He also seemed too out of breath and weak to speak a sentence without having to take several breaths between each word and then blowing out forcefully between words. His voice was low and gravelly. We had changed his meds again, and I thought perhaps he was having side effects from the new ones. In my research, I learned that with temporal lobe seizures, 95 percent of patients experience little to no help from any medication.

One evening while getting ready for bed, I found him sitting on the edge of the bed, looking very distressed. I calmed him, and he tried to sleep. Finally, he got up and sat in his office chair, slumped over, and complained about water coming out of his nose. I couldn't get him to define what was going on, and he became irritated when I tried to help him. He told me he would be OK, that he just wanted to sit up for a while.

I couldn't sleep the rest of the night, as I continued to check on him every few minutes. He seemed to feel better sitting up, but it scared me to see him like this. He seemed to rally again the following morning.

This whole incident sent genuine fear through me. Having it happen in the middle of the night, not knowing what to do, whether to take him to the hospital, was very scary to me. I felt so lost and alone.

June was a miracle month in many ways, though. Financially, the money never seemed to run out, despite having to buy two new tires for the car, among other things. And as things needed to be fixed, God used each event as a way to train me to handle the things that John had always taken care of. I found myself learning how to use and fix a weed eater, how to mow and edge the lawn, and how to fix the sprinkler system.

My nephew Paul had also become a blessing in so many ways. He hung my new solar shades on the front porch, changed the air conditioner filter, and he and Heather's kids helped me around the yard many times. Linda and Mom gave me proceeds from a yard sale we had, and that went toward finishing the porch addition, which became a surprise respite place for me. I painted my porch rockers a crisp bright white and spent many pleasurable hours on them.

Every small detail of pleasant days are worth mentioning, for at this point, my life was so difficult that any joy was treasured, no matter how small or short lived.

In California, wildfires were burning out of control. Big Sur was burning. So many memories of traveling to Big Sur with John—it felt ominous somehow, prophetic. At one point, there were over fourteen hundred fires burning throughout the state. In the Midwest, devastating tornadoes, more than at any other time in history, ripped throughout the area, followed by terrible flooding, which left parts of Iowa looking like the aftermath of Katrina.

Also that year, Barak Obama won the Democratic presidential nomination; John McCain the Republican nomination. The economy took a nosedive due to the bursting of the housing bubble and the credit crisis, and America officially entered a bear market for the first time in decades, while gasoline prices shot up to over $4 a gallon. New construction screeched to a halt; small businesses went under and banks closed. Old lending institutions failed, and it felt like the world was toppling along with the United States.

In Israel, an Israeli Arab seized an earth mover and began mowing down cars, pedestrians, and buses right in the middle of Jaffa Street, just outside the Old City where I had walked only a short time ago. World tension was at an all-time high, and President Bush made fewer public appearances. Because of the rise in oil and the falling US dollar and economy, an amazing and terrifying turn of events appeared to be on the horizon.

If anyone had told me this would happen in my lifetime, I would have laughed. Yet, here we were—in the most unstable world—prophecy happening right before our eyes. There was an ominous feeling in the air, as though everyone knew we were witnessing the end of this once great nation and the beginning of the last days. At home, I was also experiencing the last of the last days, although I didn't know it.

CHAPTER FORTY-NINE

The MMSE

(Journal Entry 06/30/06)

*I took John to the neurologist. He scored a 3 on the MMSE.
Last year at this time he was still scoring 29/30. He knows the
answers, but can't process the questions fast enough.*

People with Alzheimer's, don't know the answers, aren't oriented to
time, places, events, or people. John was very oriented, but his brain
worked in slow motion to process the question and formulate the answer.
The MMSE is designed to test true memory loss, and the questions are
asked rapidly. But John knew where he was, what day it was, what year and
month. He knew who the president was and even who was running for
president. In his lucid moments, he could point to the planets, and though
he fumbled for the names, he knew what they were and pointed them out
to me, as he had always done. Ask him a complicated question and give
him time to process, and he would answer the question. Yet, his brain was
dying, his brain stem was dying, and no one knew why. In many ways,
his memory, understanding, and awareness seemed much improved than
it was even a year ago. But, the brain stem was shutting down. Why?

I asked the doctor a point-blank question: when will I know it's time
to call in hospice? After the examination, he looked me directly in the eye
and said, "The answer is *now*."

He also confessed to me that he had been wrong: he thought he could
control the seizures and get the dementia under control. So, here I sat
across from a foremost expert on dementia—a man who wrote a book on

the subject—and he could not tell me what had happened to my husband or why he was dying.

Driving home, it felt like someone had pulled an invisible plug and everything drained out. I then realized knowing it and hearing it spoken were vastly different things. It was as though I was suddenly thrust back in time and finding out all over again that John was ill, that he was not going to live.

I didn't have time to process this new information, however. Once we returned home, I made the dreaded call to hospice. They came for the evaluation and got him enrolled. The following day, John's cousin Julie and Aunt Doris came from Maryland for a visit. This was July 4, one of my favorite holidays. I was in a daze when they arrived, not up to entertaining at all, but I was glad to have them here, and John was very happy they were coming. That Saturday I also got a letter from John's health insurance carrier, which was somehow linked to his Social Security disability plan. It turned out they no longer had funding for his health-care program, and it would be discontinued by July 15. Fortunately, hospice was now covering all of his meds.

We had gone to the mall. I was concerned about John, but he insisted on going. Later, he had a choking incident, which scared me to death, and I realized that any overstimulation would cause him to become anxious. This could happen at any time due to his difficulty in swallowing. When we got home, I called hospice to tell them, and the woman strongly urged me to keep him as calm as I could.

This proved difficult with company here, and he so wanted to take his favorite drives. We managed to keep him calm for the remainder of their visit, however. My niece Heather called during their visit. She said that she understood the feelings of pressure when having company and not knowing what to cook, so she invited all of us down to dinner. More and more, I was finding there were people who knew exactly what I needed and provided it for me before I even knew I needed it. That was so like God to do that.

At midnight that same night, I woke to find John out of bed and sitting slumped over in the living room chair, struggling with severe congestion in his chest and throat. I called hospice, and they advised me to give him the morphine and another medicine, atropine, for the secretions. When I tried to give him the drops under his tongue, he refused. After much persuasion, he consented, and it seemed to help. I slept on the couch next to him, while he slept sitting up in the chair.

I slept very little, however. He was very angry that hospice was involved and resisted everything they suggested, fighting me every step of the way. After Julie and Doris left the following day, I was completely exhausted and angry. The anger was deep: anger at the medical profession for not finding out what was wrong, anger at the system that could drop us from health care like that, and anger at John for fighting me and still trying to control the circumstances with his health care by not allowing me to give him help when he needed it. He pushed me away when I loved him so much and needed to help him.

John was angry, too. Gone was the sweet temperament; he only sat and glared at me, refusing my hugs, refusing my care. If I touched him, he pulled away. This hurt deeply. At the end of it all, there were no sweet last moments, only anger.

Hospice immediately jumped in to help us get on a long-term care program, which again involved reams of paperwork to fill in and copy in preparation for phone interviews. Always the paperwork. I would not murmur, however. God had provided for John's health care from day one, and we had paid minimal out-of-pocket expenses. If we qualified for this long-term care program, I could have someone come in to help with his care, especially his hygiene, which he no longer was able to do. As fastidious a man as he had always been, this was very alarming to me. But he would not allow me to take over this part of his care.

Hospice provided volunteer help for showering, but he was so opposed to their even coming to check on his meds and health, I couldn't imagine him ever allowing anyone to bathe him. He still very much wanted to be in control of everything.

Up to this point, John still seemed unaware that he was as sick as he was. I looked on this as a blessing in some ways; I think it would have been much harder for me to watch him deteriorate if he was experiencing it with a sound mind. And, how he was deteriorating. Down to two hundred pounds now, his face was drawn, his lips were drawn downward, and he was terribly bent over due to the breathing difficulty. Still, he got up every morning, got his own breakfast, got Mom's paper, and spent time in his chair, reading his Bible and his favorite A. B. Simpson book on the Holy Spirit and A. W. Tozer's book *The Pursuit of God*. The spirit does not get dementia. He always knew exactly what he was reading.

CHAPTER FIFTY

What Is It All For?

(Journal Entry 07/22/08)

*What is it all for? Sometime in May I had been working
through the Beth Moore "Breaking Free" series. At that time
(seems so long ago now), John was very needy, sweet, reading
to me from A. B. Simpson.*

The dynamics of our relationship, complex in so many ways, sent me
back to those old memories. There was the John who loved and adored
me contrasted with the John who could never really share himself with
me. There was the conflict of John wanting me all to himself and resenting
any time I spent with my kids or family. There was always the conflict of
my involvement in teaching the Bible study, patronizing my "little ladies'
groups" and then demanding that it all come to a halt when school let out
for summer so I could devote all my attention to him.

I loved this man. I loved his great size and remember how I had felt
when his arms were around me—loved the feeling that I was secure—safe.
I loved that I was loved and accepted just the way I was. I didn't have to
be pretty for him; he loved *me*, not my looks. Our fun times— driving,
sightseeing, shopping and buying silly things to remind us of an occasion,
listening to his made-up words to songs, and laughing hilariously as we
drove with the windows down on a cool summer evening, going nowhere.
These times all made up for the bad parts. Those were the things I was
mourning again.

Going to the mall alone one day, memories flooded over me of the two of
us there, eating at the food court, taking walks around the mall for exercise.

In our house, John loved being a part of everything—the decorating, the repairs. He was so much a part of this house, and his personality was in the walls, in the photos, and the furniture. We participated in every detail of life together—we were intertwined—there was no John without me and no me without John. Or so it seemed anyway.

My prayers were that we would be one in the other part of life that I had come to love—serving the Lord. And now, though the old John was gone, suddenly he loved my kids and had deep empathy and compassion for those who were having physical difficulties or health problems. He was so concerned for Dane's foot and prayed constantly about it. He cried over our friend Tate when he had a stroke and over another acquaintance when he began having health problems. It was as though John's own illness created this profound compassion for others who were suffering, a compassion John had never had. But why now? Why did it take this devastating disease to bring out this compassion?

All outside activity had stopped for me now. My days were filled with waiting and watching. I felt so inadequate and incompetent taking care of him. He still would not let me help him and resented it when I tried. I knew this was part of the disease, but it hurt so much. I remember the summer of 2005, when all of this had become real, and Jesus spoke the words, "Will you lay it all down for John?" I had no idea what that meant. Now I did. I couldn't allow myself to think of what Jesus had planned for my life after this was over, for now there was just isolation, loneliness, idleness, and watching John doze as he watched HGTV reruns. There was no longer any conversation. It was taking such a toll on me emotionally that I feared I might never recover. But, it was what Jesus had chosen for me.

(Journal Entry 7/23/08)

Oswald Chambers writes:

The Spirit of God in the process of sanctification will strip me until I am nothing but "myself." That is the place of death. Am I willing to be "myself" and nothing more— no friends, no father, no brother, no self-interest—simply ready for death? (Chambers, Oswald. *My Utmost for His Highest*. Ulrichsville, OH: Barbour Publishing, Inc. 1963, p. 205)

In my "pre-dementia" romanticized view of sanctification, I would have said, "Yes, Lord!" But death is agony. Death is excruciating. I was experiencing many deaths: death of my entire twenty-three years of life with John, death of John himself, death of ministry, death of freedom to come and go or to have any control over my life, death to self in every respect.

At this moment, I experienced no joy in any of it. Nor was I experiencing the nearness of Jesus. He seemed to be walking ahead of me—an unfamiliar friend. I saw no light at the end. No life at all.

Yet, I choose to say, nevertheless, not my will but thine be done.

CHAPTER FIFTY-ONE

John Is Home

(Journal Entry 7/28/08)

And now begins a new path—a new journey—unchartered territory. John, my dear, beloved husband, my bear, died at 12:25 a.m., Saturday, July 26. I am a widow.

For several days, he had been telling me he thought it was time for him to go to hospice. On Monday, July 22, after he consented to have a shower with the help of the volunteers, I took him for a haircut and then to In & Out Burger at his request. He ate a full meal and then wanted to drive to Dewey, where he knew our hospice was located. So, I drove him out there, even though I knew that it was only an office. Apparently, he thought there was a hospital or someplace he could go. When we got there, all he did was stare ahead.

I never knew what was going on in his mind, and that day was no different. The day was cloudy and cool, raining off and on, and we drove with all the windows down like we always used to do.

On that Tuesday evening, I was busying myself in the back bedroom when Greg Conrad, a good friend from church, called to see if John and I would like to come for dinner that Friday. I took the phone in to John and told him who was calling, but he very angrily said "No!" I said good-bye to Greg, and after hanging up, I told John again that it was Greg who had called, his Bible study teacher. He again retorted "No!" saying he didn't know anyone named Greg. He seemed not to even remember the Bible study. He looked different; he seemed to look through me. He said his head and his back hurt, and he wanted to go to hospice.

Alarmed, I called the nurse. She said he needed a higher and longer-lasting dosage of morphine and that she would try to get him into a five-day respite bed at a care center. I got him to bed. I, too, went to bed but didn't sleep much, as I knew something new was happening.

The following morning he got up as usual, read his Bible, ate his cereal, and watched the weather. The nurse came and arranged for him to go to a care center for five days. He was excited to go. He wanted to go. It was as if he knew something was going to happen. He *knew.*

In retrospect, I could see that he knew he was going to die. I was to take him at 4:00 that afternoon, and I wanted Dane and Linda to go with me. I was scared, not sure how I could stand to leave him in a nursing home. He didn't belong there really, as he was still walking, eating, and aware of his surroundings.

As we entered the parking lot, it was clear he knew where he was. He said this was not the right place, and he didn't want to stay. Dane, Linda, and I had to persuade him to go in, and when we got inside, he was very unhappy, very anxious. He wanted to go home. It was awful. But I was doing what I was "supposed" to do: have a five-day respite.

Everyone assured me that it was the right thing to do—for John *and* for me. So, I pushed past my gut, which told me to get him out of there. I hated it! I hated leaving him there. But I was supposed to have a respite. (Note to self: Never tell a caretaker they have to take a respite if their gut tells them not to.)

Dane and I then went to Linda's. She had ordered comfort food, and we sat a long while on her front porch.

I got home around 9:00 p.m., not feeling anything near to respite. The phone rang at 9:30. It was a nurse from the care center. She told me John wanted to talk to me, and she put him on. He mumbled something incoherent and the phone disconnected. I was distraught. Why would I leave my husband there? I determined that the next day I would find another place, an actual hospice home. I was angry with myself for not doing my homework on this one, not preparing for this ahead of time. The following morning, I went to a beautiful hospice care facility and agonized that I had chosen without checking out the alternatives.

I drove to the care center to take John his pillows and photo books. What I found was horrifying. The man who walked in the day before now looked like all the other patients—slumped over, drooling, unable to be aroused. I went into full-blown alarm. I called Linda and Dane, who rushed to my side. Talking to the nurses about what had happened, I was able to piece together some of the previous night's events. He had gotten dressed at 1:00 a.m. and gone to the nurses' station, ready to go home. They finally got him back to bed around 3:00. At 5:30, they gave him the new morphine dosage, and it took him completely into unconsciousness. They couldn't get his oxygen levels normalized, even at six liters.

I got the hospice nurse to come right away. I had to get him out of that place; he had received poor care. The volunteers who had bathed him earlier in the week also came, thinking they would give him a bath, and they, too, were shocked. I was so grateful they were there, because as John began to rouse from his deep sleep, he tried to get out of bed, and they were able to help tremendously.

The hospice nurse got the discharge papers in order, but it would be several more hours before we could leave. I got him into a wheelchair, still slumped over and drooling. No help was offered by the care center staff, and it was still very murky as to exactly how he had reached this state.

We finally got him home via hospice transport, and the nurse came for around-the-clock monitoring. The whole thing was a nightmare. The nurse ordered a hospital bed and higher oxygen. The day he went into the care center he was taking 1.5 liters of oxygen and could do well without it; now he was on 6 liters and began to lose consciousness if he was off of it. What had happened? In my mind, I believed that once he came out of the drug-induced state and was in his own bed again, he would be back to where he had been before we took him to the care center.

Getting him into the hospital bed was difficult. He was in such a deep sleep, unable to stretch out and relax. Throughout the day, Dane, Paul, and the rest of us had to hold him down, as he would rouse himself and try to get up. The nurse put Depends on him—oh, God, John in a diaper! It was all too unreal. The hospice nurse told me I should call anyone who might want to see him for the last time, as he was dying. He's dying? This can't be happening.

Pat got there as soon as she could and then Adam and Jeniece. The day stretched into the late night, and I finally went to sleep for a short time. At one point after I had fallen asleep, the hospice nurse thought John's respirations were dropping and had them wake me up. I held him, crying, but he rallied. We all finally got to bed.

I woke early, showered, and got the coffee on, feeling good in a strange sort of way. I sent e-mails to everyone I knew about John's situation. Pat and Linda came back, and I had a strange joy—even rejoicing for some reason. The house filled up with family—kids, grandkids, Mom, sisters, and our dear longtime family friend Chris Ratajski. Chris simply took charge and started cleaning, doing dishes, cleaning the bathrooms, changing sheets, and doing laundry. I felt as though I were watching from somewhere else, and I was amazed at how everyone easily moved into what they did best, like a well-choreographed dance. Linda, always knowing exactly what to feed a crowd, went with Chris to buy food for the many people who would be coming, while Pat gathered everyone around and we prayed. As soon as she and Adam prayed, I knew that everything was going to be all right. The air cleared in the house. Dane and Adam hovered around me and watched over me, protectively. Mom was in and out, aching for me, loving me.

Joe came that afternoon, and we filled the house, sitting on the front porch and the back porch, doing what we always do in a crisis: laughing and telling family stories. Eight years ago, it was Dad stories as he lay dying; six years ago, it was Jennifer stories. Now, it was John stories, and there were plenty of them. I imagine that John, just inside the door listening, was laughing, too, as he overheard the conversations.

Jeniece sat by John's side, reading to him from his Bible all the passages he had highlighted. It was a continuous round of everyone doing what they do, either through the gift of the Holy Spirit or just natural ability, and I felt held and buoyed up. Mom sent out a prayer chain notice and asked for prayers that he wouldn't linger, and I secretly asked God to take him before everyone had to return home.

Nat came, bringing a huge cake, and she and Linda went to the store to buy enough dinner for the crowd. Pastor Chris Inman came and prayed with us. With all the bustling activity, there lay John in the middle of it all, unconscious and dying. It was surreal. He would have hated it. It was a family swirl, and he always only barely tolerated our family swirls. Now, he could not escape, and I am certain he knew.

As the day wore on, Dane managed to veer the traffic out of the living room and kept it quiet. The nurse left around noon, and Linda took over John's meds and monitoring. As it turned out, that in itself was sent by God. She moved right into nurse mode. Kim, back from her camping trip, also moved into nurse mode, bringing her oximeter to measure John's oxygen levels and pulse. Almost everyone on the back porch was cutting up and laughing. I spent time there, laughing. Then, I would come inside and sit by John and speak to him, telling him how much I loved him, what a wonderful husband he had been to me.

A short time later, when I went alone into my room and saw his dresser—all the notes I had left him when I had gone to Israel still stuck to his credenza, where he had put them—I cried in bitter agony. John! How could this happen? What will I do without you?

Kim thought he probably wouldn't live more than twenty-four hours; I didn't think he'd last the night. I slept about an hour, listening to everyone still on the porch and silently thanking God for my amazing family. What a comfort they were!

I got up, probably around 10:30. Everyone began clearing out around 11:00 or so. Finally, it was just Adam, Jeniece, Dane, Linda, and I. Linda was now my hospice nurse. As soon as everyone had gone, John's pulse began to rise, and his oxygen saturation began to drop. He began Cheyne-Stokes breathing, and we all stood, holding onto his hands. We seemed transfixed, in a place between life and death. It seemed an eternity and then, at 12:25 a.m., Saturday morning, July 26, my beloved life companion and love was gathered into the arms of Jesus for his homecoming with Dad and Jen.

I heard someone let out a long, mournful wail and realized it was me. I have never felt such intense pain. It was as if someone else sat by the bed, not me. This wasn't really happening to me. But it was me and I felt inconsolable. Now came the "bubble" of that immediate period of time between death and grief where you feel as if you are walking through the process in an invisible bubble, fragile, but protected somehow.

The rest of the family returned right away. The nurse came back, and by 3:30 a.m. all of the details of a life-ending had been conducted; the coroner had come and left with John, and it was all over. John was gone.

CHAPTER FIFTY-TWO

The Miracles and the Blessings

I watched in amazement as Dane and Paul, on that first day home, stepped in to do unthinkable things while helping the nurse. No young men should have to do such things or see them done. But they performed with grace and love, and I think I saw Jesus standing among them, washing feet.

Adam, my dear son who has so often stopped everything to pray with me over these past four years, offering not only prayer but sound advice and precious comfort, fell into what was the most natural for him—prayer, comfort, and helping. He and Dane were like two mighty angels, one on either side of me, holding me, catching me lest I fall.

Chris—bustling around, cleaning my house in the midst of a throng of people. I'll never forget seeing her walk by with the vacuum cleaner and a bottle of bleach. I'm not sure my house has ever been cleaned quite like that.

Linda—looking at the people coming and going and knowing they needed to eat! With Chris and Nat, she went about buying and preparing enough food to feed a mob. And, having been through it all herself just a few short years ago, Linda knew exactly what I needed at each moment. Her comfort from her own pain was priceless.

Pat, dropping everything and driving up as fast as she could, immediately brought a spiritual dimension into the fray, gathering us all together to pray. It felt as though the Holy Spirit had shown up to pray with groanings too deep for words. Whatever was prayed during these last hours of John's life would be answered.

And there was Mom. There is no comfort or love like that of a mother. With everyone doing everything, there was not much left for her to do, but her presence was a source of strength to me, a quiet strength that comes from also having lost a husband.

John's old friends Barry Lane, Chuck Rosenberry, and Joe Thompson came for a last visit the day before he died, and I know that John knew they were there. He would have been so pleased to have them there with him.

My dear pastor, Chris, came late in the day, and his presence reminded me that I have a church family who genuinely cared for me, genuinely loved me. We sat together by John's bed and prayed with Adam. I would come to appreciate Chris more and more over the next few days.

Tasha, my sweet daughter-in-law, could not be here as much as she would have liked because of taking care of the kids, but her presence was calming and peaceful, hugging me often and looking compassionately on my grief.

Jeniece, my other sweet daughter-in-law, worked silently behind the scenes, tidying up the kitchen, reading to John, and weeping with me. I still have the note she left on my refrigerator notepad: "Keep your eyes on Yeshua."

Thursday had been hot and humid, but Friday the clouds came. In the afternoon, it rained. Later, as I sat by John's side, God gave me a precious promise, just as surely as He had a year or so ago. The sky became dark in the east as the sun shone brightly through the clouds in the west, lighting up the trees and houses with that brilliant golden glow. I whispered to John, "Oh honey, if you could see it! Our favorite scene with the sun shining against a dark and cloudy sky—it is so beautiful! All we need now is a rainbow!" And, just as if God knew that was exactly what we needed, a rainbow appeared right over John's head.

My heart burst, and I grabbed hold of this with everything in me. I recalled that day when John had called me out to the porch to see just such a scene, but I had been crying, distraught. He had hugged me and told me that God promised in Genesis that the rainbow was His promise that everything would be OK.

This was the first time in the past three days I had felt the presence of God. I had been under the most intense attacks. The enemy accused me of dropping the ball at the end, taking care of John and then dumping him at the care center when he didn't want to go, and now he was dying. That horrible memory filled my mind after John died. I was angry. After taking care of him for four years, trying to keep his life pleasant, why at the end did I have to have that terrible thing happen? But as the rainbow appeared, it was as if Jesus held me and whispered in my ear, "That isn't Me accusing you. I am here."

Over the next several days, I heard from many people that God had allowed even that to happen. My friend, Judy, said God could have allowed it because He needed to protect me. If it were going to happen anyway, the sudden drop in oxygen and everything else that transpired, God knew if it happened while I was alone, it would have been terrifying. When I expressed these attacks to Adam and Pat, they both went into instant prayer action and peace returned.

We had prayed that John wouldn't linger, that everyone wouldn't have to return home. That prayer, too, was answered.

On the morning after John died, I woke early, and God brought to my mind the Scriptures from Isaiah 43:18–19 (KJV), we had both been given back in the summer of 2005:

> "Do not remember the former things, nor consider the things of old. Behold, I will do a new thing. Now it shall spring forth; shall you now know it? I will even make a road in the wilderness and rivers in the desert."

It was as if Jesus were standing right there with me as I read, teaching me word by word what this passage meant. I listened intently. I had been instructed at one point to let go of my memories and let God do a new thing. He would use these past four years to prepare a new way in this wilderness and rivers in this desert, and He did. He spoke to my heart, "You have been walking around with a raw, open, bleeding wound for four years and now, though you will grieve again, you will also heal."

I was reminded again that though John had begun this disease with anger just under the surface and the very real possibility of becoming belligerent, we had prayed that he would go through this with the grace of God, with sweetness. And he did.

He didn't have to go into full-time care.

He never became incontinent.

Hospice was only needed for one month.

The long-term care wasn't needed after all, and our health care ended just at the moment we wouldn't need it any longer.

His death, in the end, was quiet, peaceful, and fast.

The calls, e-mails, and cards began pouring in. That Saturday was a blur of activity. Sunday, Adam, Dane, and I went to the funeral home to make the arrangements. Linda, Pat, and Mom had already decided to cover the cost—praise Jesus. After we left the mortuary, Adam wanted to go somewhere quiet and sit together for a while. I suggested we go back to Goldwater Lake, where John, Julie, Doris, and I had been together just a few short weeks ago. It was peaceful and quiet. We sat at the same picnic table and talked and prayed. My two grown sons, so mature and strong, were now taking the role of protectors for their mother.

Then God gave me a second message. As we sat talking, an eagle soared across the lake. How many times in the past four years had He sent an eagle in my time of sorrow?

Earlier that morning, God had taken me in my regular reading to Isaiah 38:10–20. Verses 10 to 14 seemed to be especially for John: "Taken in the prime of my life … deprived of the remainder of my years … my life span is gone." Then, in verses 14 to 20, God spoke directly to my own heart: "'I mourned like a dove; my eyes fail from looking upward. O Lord, I am oppressed; undertake for me! … Indeed it was for my own peace that I had great bitterness; but You have lovingly delivered my soul from the pit of corruption … The living, the living man, he shall praise you, as I do this day.'" His presence drew very near as I read and He explained verse by verse that this was for me—now and for my future.

Adam, Jeniece, Dane, and I all went to Celtic Crossings, one of John's favorite restaurants, for lunch and then everyone left for home. I had wanted a quiet evening with Pat, Linda, and Mom, so we went to dinner at Murphy's and came back home. I had asked Pat to pray through my house—to remove every last trace of dementia—and she prayed the most powerful prayer. She also anointed me and my house, and I felt things leaving—things that had been lurking, hiding in the shadows. Linda also prayed a powerful and beautiful prayer, as did Mom. I slept a peaceful sleep that night—more than I had in months. The prayers that were going up for me were palpable. Diane prayed a beautiful prayer for me over the phone from Arkansas, where she was the day John died.

The first week alone, I walked in peace through my days (the nights, however, were hard). I had lots to do. Linda took me shopping for clothes for the memorial service. Tasha wrote John's obituary, capturing him perfectly. Friends of John's from his school, Y-Camp, college, and work called. Plants arrived, along with dozens and dozens of cards. Roger Williams, a coworker of John's, called and told me in tears of when his own wife had died—how the first week would be the sweetest memory I will have. The nearness of Christ will be remembered forever he said. "There is no proper way to grieve—like the song 'sorrows like sea billows roll,' grief will come in waves." Precious words.

At church, Karen did the bulletin, using John's favorite scene of the San Francisco Peaks, and my niece Kim put together an amazing video of John's life. As I watched it, the tears flowed freely. It was John—the old John as he once was, laughing, cutting up. It brought him back to me for a brief moment.

Our dearest and oldest friends, Rachelle and Reg, called and shared some old John memories—the plans to have an ice-cream truck, only it would be run by grouchy old men—how we had all laughed over that one; their yard sale, where John tried to get everything for nothing and complained about the prices; our memorable times at the county fair. I laughed as they recounted their fond memories.

On July 30, alone with the Lord, my reading for that day was Isaiah 40, soaring on wings of eagles, which again punctuated God's message to me about the eagles. "See! I meant that to be for you!" He seemed to say. He was very near.

Adam came back on Thursday, as did Pat. Jeniece had wanted to do a John Beard memorial dinner with Tasha, so they did it up in fine fashion—jambalya and chicken big mamou—John's specialties. All the family would be here, along with John's cousins Paul and David from Maryland and his best friend Darrell from Virginia. My dear Sunday school class brought loads of food as well, and heaps of love and encouragement. As soon as Paul, David, and Darrell arrived on Friday, the fun began. It was like having John back. Everyone was telling John stories, laughing like crazy, and my nephew Ben, caught it all on videotape. As each family arrived, I was comforted all the more.

Linda and Kim planned a huge catered dinner after the memorial service at Kim's, and again, everyone just took over, paying for everything, working like crazy to make it a special day. I was bowled over by the kindness and love poured on me. I felt buoyed on comfort, encouragement, and prayer. A friend, Katy, from Bible study did yard work, wanting my yard to look nice for all the company that would be coming. People seemed to anticipate my every need before I knew I had a need. This was the body of Christ—no need to take classes or complete a program to learn how to behave, as the Holy Spirit leads here. Everyone simply did what He directed, and everything that needed to be done was done.

The dinner at Paul and Heather's was terrific. Jeniece had faced an ordeal trying to get up here from Phoenix, in fact a few ordeals, but she pulled it off. Tasha cooked up a mess of chicken big mamou; John would have been so pleased! These daughters-in-law outdid themselves, and my heart swelled as I thought of how blessed I was to have not only loving sons but loving daughters-in-law. I was more blessed than Naomi.

Saturday, Paul, David, and Darrell took me to lunch and then to the church. But, in typical Beard fashion, we arrived just in the nick of time. Late to my own husband's funeral. John would have been pacing. Kim had put together a memorial board, and at the front of the church, Tasha and Johanna had set up John's camera, his favorite Paul Prudhomme Cajun cookbook, his aprons and chef's hat, and his favorite Yosemite photo.

The service was absolutely wonderful. It couldn't have been more perfect. Paul played "The Old Rugged Cross" on his resonator, along with one of his and John's favorite Fleetwood Mac songs, "Songbird." I was able to read my own eulogy after the video had been shown; it tied the old John to the new John. Pastor Chris gave a beautiful sermon and then many people shared their stories of John. A thunderstorm developed right in the middle of one person's story, and a loud clap of thunder shook the walls. He stopped and said, "OK, John!" It was, I later thought, how John's laugh must have sounded from heaven. Ben videotaped the service, for which I was so grateful.

At the reception, I got to meet so many of John's old friends, coworkers, and others. Diane and Guy had changed their travel plans so they could be there, and they came to the family dinner at Kim's afterward, as did John's lifelong friends Barry and Billie, and our very close friends Chris and Brad. They were family after all.

The weather at the family reception couldn't have been more perfect, and the evening lingered for hours. Paul Beard, my nephew Gene, John's longtime friend Darrell, and Paul Auer jammed on their musical instruments. Gene sang the song he wrote for me, bringing me to tears again. All the kids were running and playing in the yard; the canopies were all set up with a sumptuous array of foods. The day will forever remain etched in my memory, like an old sepia photograph from faraway times.

I knew that the abiding life teaching, which had taught me so well over the past four years, would now carry me through this new path of grieving. Learning to focus on Jesus, not dementia. Letting Jesus be my love for John, my strength in weakness, my adviser in every medical and financial decision, and oh so many ways, would now become second nature to me. "He will manage my affairs."

Thinking over the four years of the journey through dementia, I was reminded of the process of learning to walk by faith and not by sight; learning to expose every situation to Jesus, who lives in me and to finally stand back and thank Him for what He will do so that I can live life miraculously. Giving thanks in this way is the evidence of true faith.

Amen.

> And he hath put a new song in my mouth, even praise unto our God: many shall see it, and fear; and shall trust in the Lord. (Psalm 40:3 KJV)

CHAPTER FIFTY-THREE

The Grieving

(Journal Entry 8/3/08)

Now begins a new journal—a new chapter in my life—a new life full of "firsts" without John.

Adam stayed as long as he could after the service. Dane, Tasha, and the kids also came over, and they all stayed until after 9:00. It felt good, having everyone here; no one wanted to leave. It had been so long since they could just linger and feel comfortable here, without the tension of upsetting John. My Sunday school class had brought so much food. The house was filled with flowers and plants, and everything was a mess, but I didn't care. The summer evenings were cool and beautiful, and we were all finally able to relax. My friend Katy came again the next week and did more yard work. Bless her heart, how I appreciated her.

On Tuesday, my new friend Carolyn—who had bought me a massage for whenever I needed it—hosted a Bridges for Peace (BFP) reception. My friend, Judy and Dane also went. It stirred my passion again for Israel, for service in Israel.

I had gone grocery shopping that day and had my first strange experience with grief, that "stalker," as Linda had called it. When someone looked in my direction, I suddenly felt the sensation that it seemed strange someone had looked at me. I realized I felt invisible, like half of me was gone. The same thing happened at the BFP reception.

My friends looked after me. Judy invited me out to dinner that week, and a widow from church had a few widows over. (I wondered if I would ever get used to being called a widow. It just didn't seem to fit.) In the middle of the week, I picked up the death certificate. I was going to run some errands and buzz in to get them and go on to my errands. But, the grief of holding these documents hit me full on, and I experienced what Linda called the bursting of the "bubble." The bubble is where you live for the first couple of weeks, seemingly oblivious to the sadness. Then, the bubble breaks, and all of it begins to pour out.

I was not prepared for this overwhelming flood of grief, loneliness, and deep aching in my heart. I couldn't run the errands. I went to Goldwater Lake to sit, thinking that it would somehow help. There I sat, where less than a month ago I had sat with John, and his absence was like a gulf of pitch-black that threatened to swallow me alive. *How do people do this?*

Then, for some strange reason—almost as if I were feeling that as long as I was going to be swallowed up, I may as well do one more difficult thing—I went to the lookout place, where John had been fixated on going so often, to stare at the San Francisco Peaks. If this was going to kill me, and I thought it might, I would feed it. But it didn't kill me. In fact, I could sense deep inside that it was going to heal me.

I knew I was now going to have to do the necessary things—taking care of the sundry postdeath financial things—but my mind would not do it. I called a friend, Alice, who helps new widows get their financial affairs in order. She went with me to the Social Security office. I learned that I would receive John's Social Security benefits when I turned sixty on my next birthday, in May. Arizona State Retirement System benefits would take about three months to process, so I would be without income for that time. My God had taken care of me thus far, however, proving to me beyond all shadow of doubt that He would continue to take care of this widow, because He cared more for me than for the little birds, so there was no anxiety whatsoever now.

Dane and Paul, God bless them, came over and repaired my duct work in the basement, which would now bring air-conditioning and heat into the office. For the past five years, it had been ice cold in the winter and steamy hot in the summer. I was so grateful for this. Paul had become my handyman, as Dane could not do much with his broken foot. He stopped by often and did little things for me: change the heater filter, fix my sprinkler heads, drag my wind-blown garbage cans back up my steep hill on the side of the house. More than this, his and Heather's company were precious to me. I thanked God often that He placed them down the street from me.

During that first week, I took on the enormous project of moving John's things out of the office and my things in. I needed to do this, as I knew that if I didn't do it then, I would not do it at all. People advised not to make any big changes right away, but I couldn't look at John's things; the pain of it was too great. I had to make these changes. I took everything out of the office except the computers and took all of John's things out of the closet, dragging them all into a pile in the living room. I moved my filing cabinets into the closet and loaded the shelves with books and binders. The physical work felt good.

Then, I began sorting through John's things. It felt like his whole life was in those boxes—his old photo albums, along with boxes of slides and memorabilia from his childhood and college days. Much of it I had never even seen.

As I worked late into the night, a dark, foreboding oppression began to settle over the house. I was suddenly aware of a sense that I was throwing away John, his history. John had no children of his own to pass it along to, and his mother's family line ended with him. I felt he was watching me and that he was angry. He always kept his things to himself, guarding everything and holding everything as though they were priceless treasures. Now I was tossing bits and pieces of his life into the trash.

A conversation began in my mind. *Throw it away, Kathy, there is no one to pass it on to. But it is John! It is his whole life!*

John's gone. He's not coming back.

All through our marriage, I had felt that I had stolen him away from a life he had loved—a life of partying and fun with his many friends in Virginia. Now I was destroying his history—the last remnant of him. The ultimate betrayal.

By Monday, the piles in the living room were still high and seemed endless. A dark gloom settled over me. It wasn't just grief, it was a black hole of grief, and I was afraid of it. I wasn't hearing from God except for small "sound bite" messages that I would reply with, "I heard that. I know it is You," and then quickly tuck away.

Still, the overwhelming sense that I had betrayed John, even at the end of his life, even having him lying so helpless and exposed in the middle of the living room—which he would have hated—and the sense that he was watching me now and was angry at me nearly undid me.

By Tuesday morning, I knew I couldn't continue, and my grief was unbearable. I no longer felt God's presence, only John's, and it was not a good feeling.

I prayed to God, "Please let me hear something from John, let him tell me that he is all right, that he's not mad at me."

Going to church without John, another first, came all too soon. It was almost more than I could bear. On the verge of tears all the way there, I thought I would sit near the back door to make a fast exit if the flood of tears threatened to escape. But dear Katy saw me and grabbed my arm, steering me to a seat next to her, where she sat as a sentry, praying. She was a comforting presence. If she hadn't, I would have bolted for the door. But I'm glad she did. I even managed to go to Sunday school, and the tears flowed freely. So many loving people reaching out to me brought all of my grief to the surface, but I felt safe crying here among my beloved friends.

Driving home, I recalled how very important it was to John to go to Albertson's to buy a newspaper after church. He would begin reminding me of it as soon as we left home to go to church and would instruct me all the way to the store (causing me to snap at him at times, unfortunately). That morning, I deliberately drove in another direction. I didn't buy a paper. It was Dane's birthday. We didn't have a big to-do; I just took him to lunch.

The pile of John's things sat like a silent, ominous presence in my living room. I had begun to walk around it, ignoring it. My kitchen counter was also stacked high, as well as the library table and the back room. Everything was out of order. My nest was upset, so my inner self was upset. I would pick something up and then set it down someplace else. A basket of John's laundry sat right in the middle in plain sight, but I couldn't look at it; I couldn't pick it up to take it into the other room. I couldn't bear to see his clothes from the last days of his life, still with his smell in them.

Finally, I dragged everything into the back bedroom and closed the door. I would deal with it later. Mom saw the laundry and took it to her place to wash for me.

I wanted to begin teaching Bible study again, and with summer over, it was time to begin. I wanted to pick up where I had left off: teaching, discipling my women, doing normal things, the things I so loved to do. But I couldn't. I was choking. I had nothing to say. Day by day, the awful, dark pain grew. I couldn't identify it. If it were merely grief, it was like nothing I had ever experienced. It was all wrapped up in guilt, anger, fear, a desperate longing for him and his warm hugs, and a host of other emotions I couldn't identify.

That next Wednesday I had a dream. This was not an ordinary dream; in fact, I question whether it was a dream at all.

In my dream, I was lying in bed next to John, looking out my window at the stars and enjoying the cool breeze, as I always did, and listening to him breathing. Suddenly, it occurred to me that he was breathing normal, steady, deep breaths. I turned to face him, and he was awake. I exclaimed "John! You're breathing normal!" He said, "I know! I'm OK—I feel good again!" We hugged and rejoiced that he was well. My heart felt his heart beating, and his body was warm. It was a most exquisite joy, coupled with a most exquisite pain, and in my dream, I thought, *Oh, please don't do this to me. If this is not real, please, I can't bear it.*

And I woke up. I turned immediately to see if he was there, well and breathing, but he was not. I didn't feel comfort or joy, just overwhelming despair.

The next morning, I was to go to the White Mountains with Kim, Linda, Mom, and Chris to check out a camping place. Driving up that beautiful mountain, I told them of my dream. As I told them, I remembered that I had asked God to let me hear from John, and all of us realized at once that God had answered that prayer. I heard from John! He was well. He was alive. He was warm. And he hugged me!

I had been attending the Abiding Life advanced training classes at Guy and Diane's, and it was due to end the following week. Although I was not ready to return to the world of ministry, I was compelled to go to the last class, having already taken the first two. Tim Lester, the leader of the training, was from Hagerstown, and he and his wife had come to my house while John was still alive to teach the class to Pat and me, because we couldn't attend the class that weekend. I had introduced him to John and told him he was from Hagerstown and that he knew John's cousin Paul. But John was mad at me, had been mad at me since I had called in hospice so he wouldn't even acknowledge Tim when I introduced them. The old John would have loved Tim, but that wouldn't happen now.

At this training, I had difficulty even staying; my tears welled up constantly and threatened to erupt into heaving sobs. I didn't want to use the material any longer; I felt I no longer had a future without John. I had no sense of any purpose whatsoever. Back home after the first evening session, I literally erupted. I called Linda, who had become one of my emotional support systems. She had been there; she could give me blow-by-blow details of the grieving process, and it was tremendously comforting. She helped me see how the lies of the enemy had slipped into the grief and convinced me (using John's own voice) I had let John down, had abandoned him in his need at the end, had never understood what his needs were, and left him all alone in the end. The enemy was there, condemning me for all kinds of things: for not being more involved in the things John enjoyed, for caring more for my interests than for him, for being an obstacle to his spiritual growth, for robbing him of his higher education work at George Washington University, and for his moving to Arizona, leaving the Maryland he loved.

Oh Lord, what heavy weights to carry. His whole life, stashed away in that closet, was his very fun and very happy life before he met me at age thirty-seven. And now it was as though that old life was taunting me, condemning me, accusing me. So, what right did I have now to go on with my life? It was an empty, cavernous feeling. These things had been attacking me for the past week, and now they were attacking me during the conference.

On Sunday, I asked Tim if I could have a moment after the session. As I gushed out to him all the crazy emotions I was experiencing, he brought clarity to me, separating the truth from the lies. Because the "covering" of my husband was gone, Tim suggested that I call on couples, men and women, from among my friends to step in and provide the physical covering I no longer had—someone to help me with household jobs, financial things, spiritual counsel. He asked me if John were here and in his right mind, would he be angry at me for going through his things. I said most definitely yes. John never allowed me to do a thing for him, not even his laundry. He kept his past private; he kept me at arm's length with everything but what he wanted to share with me. But would he be angry at me because he would think I was doing it with an evil motive and intent to hurt him? No, he wouldn't.

And then I realized what Tim was getting at. My heart had always been to do John good, to be a helpmate to him and then to care for him in his sickness. At times, I got angry with him, impatient with him. Sometimes, I spoke harshly to him, and there were even times I wished God would take him home. But, those things did not negate the fact that my heart loved John and that I did everything I could reasonably do to make his life pleasant and comfortable. And I knew that. There were many occasions when he thanked me and told me he appreciated me—those rare times when he broke through the dementia.

The enemy's grip had been broken.

The following morning, I awoke with joy—honest to goodness, supernatural joy. The awful oppression of the week before was gone, the chains around my soul broken off. Around 8:30 in the morning, Judy called to tell me she had felt led to call John Moser of the Joshua Fund to tell him that she and I were still interested in serving with Joshua Fund in some capacity. When she mentioned my name to John, he responded, "Oh yes, we know Kathy. We have been in contact with her. My wife and I both felt a strong connection to her when we talked to her in Israel and have both felt the Lord was going to use her in this ministry. Her name comes up often around here."

My heart felt like it exploded inside of me. A year ago, I had heard from the Lord that I was to go on that trip; I had no idea why. Now it started to feel like God's plan for my life was about to be revealed, and it was the most extraordinary sensation. A week before, Pat had told me that she felt God was going to take me through the grieving process quickly, because He already had plans for my future. Judy said the same thing.

—

(Journal Entry 8/28/08)

Weeping may endure for a night; but a shout of joy comes
in the morning. (Psalm 30:5)

After that week, Jesus began ministering deep healing to my soul in so many ways. Instead of that dark grief, there was just a terrible, aching missing of John. He was everywhere I looked. But, it was not that bottomless grief that has no hope at the end. Jesus made very real to me the fact that John is with Him, whole and well. Now when I thought of John and the sadness of the last four years, I immediately turned my eyes to Jesus and rejoiced that John was alive and well, and he was not sad, brooding in a corner of the house.

Friends continued to call, and cards came in piles. Money also came in. My son Adam and his wife sent money. A friend, a widow, Joan handed me an envelope with cash in it. Judy and Darrell shared financially from their hearts, as did Aunt Doris. My dear friends Eunice and Mark felt God leading them to send me their tithe until my retirement benefits started, so every couple of weeks, I received their checks in the mail. These sustained my income for three and a half months. Larry and Sue handed me an envelope that contained enough money to carry me through nearly a month.

My sweet nephew Paul and his wife, Heather, were a great comfort and help to me, stopping by and spending time, helping me with odd jobs, and having me over to dinner. Dane stopped over between jobs several times a week, and his presence brought such joy. He, Tasha, and my beloved grandkids were able to come and spend long hours with me, filling my days with joy. Adam called frequently, offering comfort, support, and encouragement.

Mom, living downstairs, was also a great comfort. Just having her close and knowing she was there was precious. I was able to spend more time with her now.

Jesus indeed replaced the "covering" with members of my church and other good friends. One friend, Sue, took me under her wing and let me come and stay in her beautiful house in the pines while she and her husband were out of town. It was a genuine retreat. She wanted to help me with yard work, and she conspired with a group of servants of the Lord to do everything that needed to be done around my house. By the time they were finished, I had shingles replaced on the roof, my carpet shampooed, and my yard completely cleaned up. A crew from National Bank who does service for others dug up the grass and replaced it with stone. Then Sue, Diane and Guy, and landscaper, George had the remainder of the yard beautifully landscaped. Later, Sue also felt led to do an entire redo of my home, with her amazing skills in interior design.

I felt I was snuggled in a cocoon of protection made up entirely of the precious saints of the Lord. I had never before experienced such blessings. After four years of intense emotional pain, it seemed that the Lord had opened up the heavens and began raining down blessings upon me.

Adam came up in September, and he and Dane began the laborious task of going through the garage, dividing up John's tools between them without so much as a disagreement over anything. It took two full days, and when they were finished, I could finally park the car in the garage for the first time. Then they went through John's dresser drawers and moved the dresser into the back bedroom. During all of this, the old feeling that John would walk in and find us going through his things threatened to return. At church that morning, I heard the now familiar voice of my Shepherd, saying, "Kathy, it is okay to throw away John's past. That old John died—he became a new creation in Christ, and all of that stuff died with him." My heart leaped. Jesus gave me permission, and peace followed.

A week later, I still had boxes of photos and memorabilia in the back room, which I asked Tasha to come and help me sort. We spent an afternoon going through box after box, and her presence helped us turn it into an afternoon of laughter. Finally, it was done: all of the photos were sorted through. Dane and the kids came later, and I fixed up a dinner for all of us. My house felt clean and filled with light of new beginnings.

I began to hear from Jesus about my future. He spoke to me in church one Sunday that just as Anna, the widow in the book of John, had spent her widow years praying in the temple, I could now be free to do the same. From time to time, I would stay through the third service, sitting in a corner of the balcony and praying for our church.

Jesus was indeed doing deep restoration and healing in my soul, mapping out His plan for my future, and I spent my days in peace. There was grief, yes. But there was peace, side by side with it. My dear women friends, my mom, my sisters, my sons and their wives provided a haven of love, long lunches, and good fellowship. They kept my days filled beyond what I could ever have imagined or hoped. I felt I was on the other side of that cross, and as Hebrews 12:2 reminded me, "Jesus, who for the joy set before Him, endured the cross, despising the shame."

Joy is on the other side of the cross.